Scout Worship

Compiled by
Tony Coslett
The Rev. Kenneth Faulkner
The Rev. Krister Ottosson,
Valerie Peters
The Rev. John Reynolds

Illustration
Brian Gough

Editorial
P. G. Brooks
T. A. Stringer

General Editor
Ron Jeffries

First Edition
January 1975

Printed in Great Britain by

Warners
(MIDLANDS) LTD
BOURNE & LONDON

Contents

A Commendation

by Sir William Gladstone, Bt., Chief Scout of the United Kingdom and Overseas Branches

The Scout Movement has a special and important opportunity in the religious training of young people — an opportunity to relate religion to life and action in terms which boys readily understand and absorb. This is the aim which this book takes up from its first sentence: and throughout its pages it practises what it preaches. It is so packed with sound advice and helpful material that it is not easy to add anything useful to what it says. It stimulates one to think imaginatively about worship as well as providing many good examples.

Young people, as well as those adults who are concerned with their Christian upbringing, are rightly critical of the exclusive use of traditional forms of worship. The profundity and beauty of traditional forms cannot be appreciated if young people are thrown in at the deep end. But it is much easier to criticise traditional forms than it is to substitute a more modern and relevant service. This needs much thought and careful preparation. Here is a book to put us on the right lines. It is the fruit of much experience.

"The sabbath was made for man, and not man for the sabbath." Worship is a vital, changing thing, and we must help boys to realise that "the Kingdom of heaven is within you". My personal experience leads me to say confidently that in informal worship the Scout Movement is a long way ahead of most schools; and I think this book testifies to that.

Of course this book is not the last word! I hope that one of its most important contributions will be to encourage those who use it to collect and sift new material. Much modern art — whether 'highbrow' or popular — contains (as this book points out) some religious content. But, in comparison, for instance, with the Victorians, our generation is still in a great dearth of good popular religious music. Thus, whilst careful thought and selectivity are important in the composition of a service, I also appeal to those who use this book to cast their nets wide, in order that we may reap the harvest of the popular arts of today, and use them to the glory of God.

Section 1

Understanding the
Religious Policy

"In the Scout Movement we merely lay before the boys the simplest fundamental ethics of religion and then get them to put them into practice. We put them as Christ taught them in their simplest form:

Love thy God with all thy Heart;
Love thy neighbour as thy self."

Lord Baden-Powell, the founder of our Movement, laid down in these few words our religious policy. But he knew that it was quite meaningless for young people to learn pieces of text off by heart, only to recite them parrot fashion; some practical application of the two commandments was needed.

He saw Scouting as a means of teaching Love for God through the world of nature and he saw Love for your neighbour, expressed in active form by the offering of service to others, as the complement of this. These basic ideas found expression in Scouting in several ways. The introduction of the daily 'good turn' without reward, the understanding that nobody possesses a gift until he has expressed gratitude for it, the denial of 'self' in the service of others, and 'love' for others in place of 'love for self'. B.-P. believed that this fundamental approach was a step towards understanding, not a substitute for, religion.

When the Movement was originally launched B.-P. regarded it partly as an additional means by which the churches would hold their members. But it was discovered that Scouting appealed to a vast number of boys, many of whom did not belong to churches or have particular religious views.

The Scout Movement is therefore concerned both to bring within its influence boys who have no religious attachments and to provide boys who are members of churches with other ways of exploring their faith. Many changes have taken place in the Movement since those early days but its religious policy remains unaltered, even strengthened.

The religious policy is set out in full in *Policy, Organisation and Rules, Part One*, Rule 9.

"9. The Scout Movement includes members of many different forms of religion. The following policy has received the approval of the heads of the leading religious bodies in the United Kingdom:

(i) Each invested member of the Movement shall be encouraged:-

    (a) to make every effort to progress in his understanding and observance of his Promise 'To do my best to do my duty to God',

    (b) to belong to some religious body and

    (c) to carry into daily practice what he professes.

(ii)   If a *Scout* does not belong to a religious body the Scouter responsible for his training must endeavour to put him in touch with one, which should, if possible, be that to which his parents belong or into which he may in the past have been formally admitted; the approval of the parents of the *Scout* must be obtained;

(iii)   If a Sponsored (Closed) Group is restricted to members of one particular form of religion or denomination the Sponsoring Authority is responsible for the religious training of the *Scouts* and it is the duty of the G.S.L. to encourage the attendance of all members of the Group at such religious instruction and observances as the Sponsoring Authority may consider desirable.   The Sponsoring Authority, as such, is not responsible for other matters of Scout Training.

(iv)   If a Group is composed of members of several denominations or religions they should be encouraged to attend the services of their own form of religion.   Group Church Parades will not be held and any form of daily prayer or divine service in camp should be of the simplest character, attendance being voluntary.

(v)   Where it is not permissible under a rule of the religion of any *Scout* to attend religious observances other than those of his own form of religion, his G.S.L. must make certain that this is known by all leaders concerned with the *Scout's* training so that they may ensure that such a rule is strictly observed while he is under their control;

(vi)   In order to make the Warrant structure for Commissioners, Group Scout Leaders and Leaders of Training Sections more effective, the District Commissioner, or the County Commissioner in the case of Commissioners, must satisfy himself that any applicant for such an appointment is fully aware that he will be expected by his personal example to implement the religious policy of the Association.

Combined Religious Services, and Scouts' Own Services

10.   (i)   Attendance by *Scouts* of various forms of religion at a combined Service is allowed with the permission of the D.C. and religious authorities concerned.   Such attendance should be voluntary and Rule 9 (v) must be observed;

(ii)   Gatherings of *Scouts,* to be known by the term *Scouts' Own Service,* may be held for the worship of God and to promote a fuller realisation of the Scout Promise and Law.   These are to be supplementary to, and not in substitution for, the religious observances referred to in Rule 9.''

It is clear then that the Scout Movement not only has a definite religious policy, but that leaders have a responsibility to understand it and uphold it just as enthusiastically as the rest of the Scouting programme.

''Scouting does not attempt to find the lowest common factor upon which all can agree, but sets up an ideal of religion and leaves all free to interpret that ideal in their own way.''   *Scouts' Owns* by the Rt. Rev. 'Pat' Leonard.

A further point is also relevant: while this book has been written from a Christian point of view, due allowance must be made for those in the Movement who do not accept the Christian faith, but follow some other religious pattern. Like the Bible itself, our religious policy needs contemporary interpretation, so let us first consider the leader's responsibility in this context.

The Leader

As we have seen in the religious policy quoted above, "Each invested member of the Movement shall be encouraged *to make every effort to progress* in his understanding ...." This applies to all, from the youngest Cub Scout to the oldest Commissioner. It means that, taking into account the age, capability and background of the individual, he is expected to accept the Promise as the main condition of his membership and, thereafter, make continuous efforts to grow in his understanding of it. It acknowledges his need of a progressive relationship of love and service to God and others as a life-long commitment.

How a person's duty and relationship to God will be expressed depends largely on the principles of the religious faith he holds, and while many people have no firm allegiance to any particular religion, it is extremely important for anyone who wishes to fulfil a position within Scouting to try to come to a fuller knowledge and observance of religious faith. If you are going to achieve the spiritual development of young people, you must first demonstrate to them your own living faith. Otherwise, how can you be true to the aim of the Movement and honest to those whom you lead?

Spiritual exercise is just as important as physical exercise and progress in the spiritual life depends to a large extent on the exercise of prayer. The individual will also find much help and support in the active sharing with others in communal worship. The very exercise of assisting the boys in both these spheres, especially in situations which are unique to Scouting, will be most formative and rewarding.

The Boy

It is apparent that many boys come to Scouting in a spiritual vacuum. The majority of parents neglect the things of the spirit, so it is not surprising that their children have had little or no instruction in religious matters apart from what they have received at school. Here is a marvellous opportunity for the leader to stimulate an awareness of God and a satisfactory relationship with Him. It is important, therefore, for the boy to see his leader as a man of principle, with a firm faith in God and in his own purpose in life.

There are many situations in Scouting designed to encourage the boy's spiritual development. The training programmes, for example, help him to face himself and to discipline himself from within. A good leader will use the programme to introduce a spiritual aspect or attitude. As B.-P. originally said, the observation of nature can be harnessed to create a sense of wonder and admiration from which worship is but a short step.

The leader ought to relate the content of the Scout programme to the Scout Promise. For example, we teach First Aid in order that a boy can not only gain a badge, but also serve other people and through that service fulfil part of his religious obligation.

At all times leaders should be prepared to discuss their attitudes and problems in relation to life and God. Troop and camp life is full of unique opportunities for introducing topics or making comments which have a bearing on spiritual progress. We must also be convinced *and convincing* about the necessity of corporate worship.

Faith never comes to anyone automatically; it is the result of many influences: surroundings, upbringing (including religious instruction), home background and personal experience. Generally speaking, religious bodies are responsible for the 'handing on' of faith, but knowing what to believe is obviously not enough, any more than knowing the Scout Promise and Law makes a person a good Scout. Religious teachings have no life of their own until they receive the breath of faith. If a leader has a personal and living faith of his own he cannot help conveying it to others. If, however, he is unsure of his convictions and feels that he cannot help his Scouts in their growth and understanding of basic belief, he should at least refrain from expressing his own lack of faith and take positive steps to receive help from someone competent to give it. The chapter on 'Spiritual Training' will help on this.

Worship

The word worship really means the turning of a person's whole personality to God whether as a member of a religious community or alone as an individual. The worship of the particular denomination or branch of the church has first claim upon his time at the normal hours of Divine Worship.

If the Group is part of a local church or is a Sponsored Group this usually raises little difficulty, assuming that the leader has a good understanding with the minister. If he does — and he should make every effort to do so — he will naturally co-operate in the fullest possible way and the Group will worship together in the manner to which they are accustomed.

In a Group not part of a local church the leader's position is more difficult although his obligation is still the same. He may have boys in the group from different religious backgrounds and yet he is required to help them all to follow their particular religion. The leader cannot literally take them all to their respective churches. On the other hand, by being keen on his own church and by refraining from disparaging any other churches to which his boys may belong, he can help all to realise that the worship of God is of vital importance.

A wise leader should find out at once to which branch of the church or to which religion each boy belongs, and must encourage him, not only to attend his place of worship regularly and faithfully, but to take his place in the church's life and work, and to serve it actively. It must be borne in mind that not all denominations make the same demands upon their members, nor do they all give the same opportunities for service. It is the leader's duty to find out each boy's obligations and opportunities and so do all that he can to make it possible for the boys to meet them.

Style of Living

All the churches in the United Kingdom are agreed as to the value of the Scouting 'method' of character training and are happy to allow their boys to receive a code of behaviour and conduct that will help them to make the highest possible contribution to the community of which they are a part.

Nevertheless, any form of religion which is based purely on 'good works' will fail unless it has its counterpart in worship. Similarly Scouting, if it was based solely upon a code stemming from the Scout Law, would be wholly unsatisfactory. Fundamental principles alone should guide us here; 'Love God' must always come first. The first clause of the Promise makes this quite clear.

For many young people attendance at church is a stumbling block; they will say that they get nothing from it and that it doesn't help them. But it is not always possible to know what we get, or will get, from going to church, and in any case the 'what do I get out of it?' approach is not really the right one. The reason for going to church is to worship God, and it is thus one of the ways in which we fulfil our Duty to God.

'Duty', however, is often thought of as being somewhat necessary yet unpleasant; for many young people it is to be avoided at all costs! But in a religious context it underlies the pleasure and joy of gathering with others who share the same faith and love in regular worship. The aim of training in Duty to God is to help every boy to attain full membership of a church; either the one to which he is already attached or one of his choice. It should not be difficult for a Cub Scout to relate the meaning of 'duty' to his own family background. This interpretation of the Promise can then be expanded progressively to the growing individual.

Church Parades

Every Group works within its own local and district situation which naturally includes the churches. Many Groups have a normal and helpful relationship with a particular church and it may well be the custom to hold church parades at regular intervals. In the light of current thinking however, we need to discuss the differing points of view concerning Church Parades and come to a sensible conclusion after thought, discussion and experiment. The following comments are offered for consideration:

(1) The relationship between the Group and the church is of crucial importance. Leaders of both should seek to establish good relationships and informed understanding. The phrase Duty to God should be given meaning both through the weekly programme of the Group and the Group's relationship with the adult community of the church. Church Parades are not a substitute for this relationship.

(2) Most leaders will want to encourage young people to attend the appropriate church regularly. However those who take sufficient interest in their local church will quickly appreciate the irritation that too frequent Church Parades cause among the church's teaching staff.

(3) As a general rule, Church Parades should be held only when there are good reasons for holding them. In one church this meant holding a monthly Parade or family service. In this instance, the young people were helped in understanding the integration of their

Group into the church's life by the Parade. Another church decided that the holding of Parades on Sunday mornings caused too many problems for the Sunday School and Junior Church departmental staff! They, therefore, held the Parade on Sunday evenings and this has been judged successful by all concerned. Some churches have abandoned Church Parades altogether. This can be done satisfactorily as long as other ways can be found of expressing the purpose of Church Parades.

(4) Many churches now limit Church Parades to the two or three occasions in the year when everyone worships together in a special Festival Service. (Christmas, Easter, Harvest etc.) Because these services are planned with the whole congregation in mind there is not the special problem of catering for a group of young people within an adult congregation.

It will be appreciated from the above that Church Parades, however venerated by tradition, must not be taken for granted and must be thought out afresh, imaginatively and creatively.

In summary: (a) The holding of Parades at whatever frequency should be worked out in close consultation with the relevant religious body and should express a relationship that already exists, rather than be a means of creating relationships.

(b) In deciding the time and frequency of Parades, bear in mind the Sunday School or Junior Church departments and the total educational programme of the church.

(c) The feelings and thoughts of the young about Parades should be treated with respect.

(d) It may be right not to hold Parade Services.

(e) If holding a Parade Service is a point of dispute try to make it a point of creative tension for both young and old, by exploring the fundamental issues, so that it can become a point of growth rather than a tension which divides the Group from the church.

(f) Where a boy belongs to a Group in a church other than where he normally attends, he should not be expected to attend that church for Church Parades, providing he is regularly in attendance at his home church. This principle also applies where boys are of another faith. No coercion of any kind should be brought on such boys to attend these Parades and if in any doubt, parents' permission must be given. It must be recognised, however, that because of their sense of loyalty to their Group, such young people may want to attend Church Parades.

Scouts' Own Services

A Scouts' Own Service is not an obligatory part of the Scout Programme and in the Church Group there may be less need of it than in others. This is a matter which must be decided between the minister and leader concerned. There must, for instance, be no clashing of times with church services. Camp provides a very suitable occasion for a Scouts' Own and has a special value which will be dealt with in a later chapter.

Weekend Camps

The practice of holding a number of weekend camps has unfortunately been the cause of criticism on the part of certain ministers who, for one reason or another, have resented the absence of their boys from their own services. This may be due either to a failure on the part of the leader to consult with the minister, or a failure on the part of the minister to appreciate the benefits that come from a properly organised and well run weekend camp.

The wise leader should take every opportunity to discuss the matter with his minister well beforehand and should explain the reasons for the camp and the effect of it as far as Scouting is concerned. It must always be remembered, however, that the final decision in the case of Sponsored Groups is in the hands of the Sponsoring Authority. In other Groups, provision has to be made for freedom in regard to religious obligations, and no boy should be taken to a weekend camp if his parents or minister raise objections and maintain them after the matter has been discussed.

Section 2

Exploring
Acts of Worship

Communal worship should express the significant feelings of a particular community of people, in our case normally a gathering of Scouts, and therefore the content of an act of worship should draw on the whole of life. Our ideals, feelings, hopes and failures should all come into our worship as should our society, the way in which we live, and the future.

Unfortunately, because the practical application of the Duty to God part of the Scout Promise is so difficult, it is easy for us to say that the boy of today has no feeling for religion and that therefore we need take no trouble over the preparation of a religious observance for young people. But the truth is quite the opposite upon taking a closer look at the aspirations and needs of young people. In this materialistic world there is amongst young people a spiritual awakening which although taking many forms, is in every case motivated by a sincere and deep concern for society. In the music of the young, for instance, there is a wealth of spirituality of one type or another and conversation and experiments in the field of after-life, mysticism and the meaning of existence are at their height.

Here, therefore, is a wonderful opportunity for all those who profess a faith. Worship is — or should be — one of the ways practising Christians express their joy at being alive; a magnificent shout for God, loud enough for the whole world around us to hear. Sadly, many Christian acts of worship are not like this and as merely expressions of adult feeling they leave little room for participation by young people.

A large number of adults fear that young people will indulge in unusual methods of worship, as they do in their musical and clothing tastes. They believe that this trend is better discouraged and therefore anything which does not conform to the accepted pattern of worship is not really acceptable. This attitude is born out of a concern and love for the worship traditions we have inherited and which provide us with a close link to the Christians of the past. But it tends to ignore the fact that worship has evolved over many centuries and has never stood still. As then, worship today should reflect our contemporary life and it would be a pity if our expression of belief was held back by the traditions of yesterday.

At the other extreme is the outlook that anything more than five years old is out of date and must be discarded as old fashioned. This approach is likely to fail as is a service taken directly from the Book of Common Prayer. The whole idea of 'fashions' is totally meaningless in the context of worship. The content and sincerity of a service are the important factors and in this respect a church organ can have as much effect on young people as a pop group. On the other hand, the new media offer leaders and clergy a unique chance to communicate to young people that Christianity is a real celebration of living.

The Use of Talents

In worship you must not be afraid to use the talents of the individual. There is a tendency for all forms of Christian worship, including Scouts' Own Services, to rely on the person's ability to sing, play a musical instrument or think deeply as in prayer. This does not give those who are unable to sing or to read out loud a chance to offer their talent to God and therefore we should be prepared to encourage the participation in worship of people who, for instance, may be able to paint or draw and could illustrate parts of the address or the reading, or even the prayers. We should encourage young people to use their musical instruments in worship and we should not label this 'gimmickry'. It is merely a sincere attempt to give everyone a chance to offer themselves and their talents to God through the act of worship.

Popular songs often carry a message which could be used as the basis for an address or service theme — and no service should be without an underlying theme. Since Simon and Garfunkel recorded *Bridge Over Troubled Waters* this haunting song has been included in many services, often performed by a solo artist accompanied on guitar. Contemporary music is therefore an acceptable and good source of inspiration for an act of worship and should certainly be borne in mind by anyone thinking of running a service for young people. Those leaders who feel unable to choose suitable records from the pop culture would be wise to consult their boys who would no doubt respond with enthusiasm providing the approach was made in a sensible way. Pop groups can also be used effectively, providing they are rehearsed and that the music they are asked to play is within their scope and capabilities.

Where hymns are concerned it is true to say that our imaginations often extend little further than *Onward Christian Soldiers* and *Holy, Holy, Holy*. Beautiful as they both are it is easy to fall into the way of believing the boys will never tire of singing them and other 'routine' hymns. Unfortunately we often take little trouble to use new hymns and tunes simply because we do not know any or are afraid that they will not go down well. There is no reason to part completely with an old and respected favourite but this is no excuse for not seeking out fresh material that will stimulate religious interest in young people.

Use of Prayer

Corporate prayer is usually the greatest imposition ever forced on boys. Adults prepare long lists of prayers and thoughts on what they think are suitable subjects or, at the end of a meeting, prayers are said without any preparation at all. As a consequence of both actions all meaning is lost, particularly when the only source of direction would seem to come from the old *Scout Prayer Book.*

When adults lead prayers and it is really necessary to use a book, it is worthwhile spending some time choosing one to which the boys can relate. The prayer book market is an ever increasing one but some old favourites like *Interrobang* by Norman C. Habel and *God Thoughts* by Dick Williams are still as valuable today as they ever were while *Scout Prayers*, published by The Scout Association, provides a more recent compilation of suitable material.

It is not always easy to find things which will be relevant and meaningful in worship for young people. The answers can only come after a great deal of searching and hard work involving the participation of the young people themselves. It is particularly valuable in this instance to encourage the boys to write their own prayers thus stimulating a personal relationship with God in familiar terms rather than one founded on outside direction.

Use of Camp Fire Spirituals

So many Camp Fires turn quite naturally 'spiritual' towards the end. Often a distinct change of atmosphere takes place encouraged by the sort of song which is sung: *My Father's House, Kum Bah Yah, Softly at the Close of Day* (most can be found in the *Faith, Folk and Clarity* series), and by the short talks given by a leader. Because these are natural expressions of feeling their effect is all the greater. Perhaps therefore, if the Camp Fire is held on a Saturday evening, there could be no need for a Scouts' Own Service on the Sunday.

Many leaders may have experienced the occasions when, during a hike or camp, particularly with older Scouts and Venture Scouts, conversation has turned to deeper subjects leading up to a questioning of the leaders' beliefs. Here is another natural opportunity which should not be ruined by a forced Scouts' Own, unless it can successfully carry on what has already taken place.

Choosing a Reading

We deal with this point in some detail later on and offer a small selection of readings which are easy to find and explain. The field of literature offers a rich variety of suitable readings for a service; Dickens for example, provides many instances of social insufficiency whilst Ernest Gordon's *Miracle on the River Kwai* and Coretta Scott King's *My Life with Martin Luther King Jr.* provide wonderful illustrations of true Christian love in terrible and frightening situations. If each leader were to consider his own reading material he would probably find many books carrying a strong message which could be interpreted at a service. Poetry, too, is a useful stimulus for thought and there are many books available on the market — *Stepney Words* edited by Chris Searle and *Love More or Less* by Sydney Carter are just two examples.

There are a number of anthologies of items for readings available such as *Words for Worship* edited by Christopher Campling and Michael Davis and whilst they are usually expensive to purchase they can always be obtained from a library — or even a local clergyman. Leaders should really look over a wide field when choosing their material ensuring that what they do choose is in some way related through a theme: hymns, prayers, readings, all relevant to each other and the aim of the service.

Implementation—an Act of Worship

At the National Scouters' Conference in 1972, The Scout Association used a service which took into account not only a theme — 'the boys in today's world' — but also the venue, a large pentagon shaped hall, and all that it offered in acoustics and lighting. Darkness, coloured spotlights, bright and dimmed lights were all used to make the service a real expression of joy. Reactions were mixed but as an example it is useful, particularly as poetry, drama, a different form of Biblical presentation, modern and traditional hymns were all used and inter-related.

The service began with a period of silence for private meditation during which a suitable piece of recorded music was played to assist thought and prayer and all lights were darkened except for a white spotlight trained on a cross specially designed for the service and hung in a prominent position. A young Scout read the prologue (and epilogue) to a congregation sitting in total darkness whilst he was spotlighted. The darkness was continued during the call to worship, except that the robed choir was illuminated by a blue light. Over all, twelve people, including two ministers who were leading the service, were involved in the actual presentation. Scouts, Venture Scouts and leaders all participated together.

To assist you in understanding the progress of this service the technical details are given as you read through, but it should be borne in mind that if you decide to use the service for yourself, a rehearsal of all the participants is necessary. On the other hand there are simpler forms of presentation which are equally successful and a good example of such a service can be found in the chapter dealing with 'Themes'.

Act of Worship

Theme—The boy in today's world

Introduction (all lights out — spotlight on cross)

Before our act of worship begins there will be a short space of time set aside for private prayer and meditation during which the *Allegri Miserere* will be played. Through this period consider in depth your work with young people, and especially your knowledge of the society in which they are growing and the many influences in their lives.

In prayer ask God's guidance on your work for the coming year and give thanks for his blessings over the past twelve months.

Prologue (spotlight on Scout)

I am just a boy
with a lot of dreams
but what's the point
I won't get nowhere
I'm just ordinary
nothing special just
. . . . ordinary
got no chance in this
world unless you're
. . . . clever
which I'm not.

Taken from *Stepney Words: (Poem by a fourteen year old boy).*

Call to Worship (faint lighting generally — spotlights on choir)

Psalm 150, sung by the choir to Charles Stanford's arrangement.

O praise God in his holiness; praise him in the firmament of his
    power
Praise him in his noble acts; praise him according to his excellent
    greatness
Praise him in the sound of the trumpet; praise him upon the lute and
    harp
Praise him in the cymbals and dances; praise him upon the strings
    and pipe
Praise him upon the well-tuned cymbals; praise him upon the loud
    cymbals
Let everything that has breath; praise the Lord.
Glory be to the Father, and to the Son, and to the Holy Ghost.
As it was in the beginning, is now and ever shall be
World without end.   Amen.

Hymn of Praise (all lights on)

O Worship the King

    O Worship the King
    All Glorious above;
    O gratefully sing
    His power and His love;
    Our Shield and Defender,
    The Ancient of Days,
    Pavilioned in splendour,
    And girded with praise.

(please sit)

Prayers of Thanks (the minister then says—)

Friends, we are gathered here to offer our whole selves to God
through Our Lord Jesus Christ; to dedicate ourselves anew to the
Brotherhood of Scouts, and to remember the true purpose of our
calling as leaders of boys and young men.
    Remembering that Jesus said 'Where two or three are gathered
together in my name, there I am among them', let us now direct our
thoughts and prayers to God assured that his Holy Spirit is with us.

You are asked to remain seated and to join in the responses
(led by Scout Leader)

V. We thank you, Lord, for our involvement with young people.
R. And for the privilege of working with, and for them.
V. We thank you for the trust they place in us.
R. And for their friendship and confidence.
V. We thank you for Scouting and its programme of fun and
    adventure.

R. And for the foresight of our Founder which made the programme possible.

V. We thank you, Lord, for all the Scouts we lead, have led, and will lead.

R. And for all those who share in their lives.

Prayer of Confession (the minister then says—)

In the confidence of his love, let us confess our faults to Almighty God and before each other saying—
(All remain seated and say together)

Almighty God, our heavenly Father
We have sinned against you,
Through our own fault
In thought, word and deed
And in what we have left undone.
For your Son Our Lord Jesus Christ's sake,
Forgive us all that is past;
And grant that we may serve you
In newness of life
To the Glory of Your name.   Amen.

(Reproduced with the permission of the Registrars of the Convocations of Canterbury and York)

The Absolution (the minister then pronounces the Absolution)

(A Commissioner, two leaders and a Venture Scout now lead our thoughts)

Prayers of Acknowledgement and Intercession
Reflection on the Pressures on Young People

Commissioner — We acknowledge, Lord, that Scouting, no matter how important we believe it to be, is only one small part of a boy's life, and that for most of the time he is influenced and guided by others.

Scout Leader — His home environment provides:

Venture Scout — My parents, family, neighbours — and friends.

Scout Leader — His school, college or university provides:

Venture Scout — My teachers, tutors, counsellors — and friends.

Scout Leader — His place of employment provides:

Venture Scout — My employer, customers, workmates — and friends.

Commissioner — And to each of these institutions and to every one of these people, the boy must devote much of his time and loyalty.

Cub Scout Leader — But Lord, many of the influences on the boy are not necessarily good. Many of the pressures of our modern industrial and technological society can cause mental and physical harm.

The folk group will now sing *Feeling Sad and Lonely* by Sydney Carter. Listen to the words and read them, and ask God to strengthen you as you try to lead young people to a sense of right and worth in today's materialistic society.

Feeling sad and lonely?
Drinka pinta milka day
Love is sure to come your way
Drinka pinta milka day.

Chorus

We don't want your money,
Honey,
We just want to do you good.

Feeling sad and lonely?
Smoke this sexy cigarette
Girls are not so hard to get
If you smoke this cigarette.

Chorus

Feeling sad and lonely?
Why not start a bank account?
See the way the stock will mount
If you have a bank account.

Chorus

Feeling sad and lonely?
Why not buy a racing car?
Pretty girls are never far
If you've got a racing car.

Chorus

Feeling sad and lonely?
It's the truth we're telling you
It is not pork sausages
It is love we're selling you.

Chorus

(please remain seated as our prayers continue)

Commissioner — Lord, we are coerced by the pressure of advertising into buying goods we could do without. Lord, this is particularly harmful to the young for whom money is often short as they strive for the qualifications which our society demands from them.
Scout Leader — We pray that we may grow in our understanding of the society in which young people are living. Help us, Lord, to understand the pressures on their lives. Help us to consider the demands on their time, that together with those who share in their lives, we may strive to encourage the physical, mental and spiritual development of young people.

The Lord's Prayer (lighting dimmed — red lights played on congregation)

The folk group will now lead us in singing the Lord's Prayer to the Caribbean setting. You are particularly asked to join in the chorus of 'Hallowed be Thy name', but if you are able to sing the whole, then please join in.

Our Father who art in Heaven,
    Hallowed by Thy name,
Thy Kingdom come, Thy will be done,
    Hallowed be Thy name,
On the earth as it is in Heaven,
    Hallowed be Thy name,
Give us this day our daily bread,
    Hallowed be Thy name,
Forgive us our trespasses,
    Hallowed be Thy name,
As we forgive those who trespass against us,
    Hallowed be Thy name,
And lead us not into temptation,
    Hallowed be Thy name,
But deliver us from all that is evil,
    Hallowed be Thy name,
For Thine is the Kingdom, The Power and the Glory,
    Hallowed be Thy name,
For ever and for ever and ever,
    Hallowed be Thy name,
Amen, Amen, it shall be so,
    Hallowed be Thy name,
Amen, Amen, it shall be so,
    Hallowed be Thy name.

The Scout Law (all lights on)

You are asked to stand and to say together each Scout Law and then to listen to the Biblical quotation which follows.

All repeat: A Scout is to be trusted.

St. Paul, in writing to the Corinthians, said 'We want you to do what is right for we have no power against truth but only for it'.

All repeat: A Scout is loyal.

John said to the church elder, 'My dear friend, you show a fine loyalty in everything that you do for these our fellow Christians, strangers though they are. They speak of your kindness. Please help them on their journey, in a manner worthy of God.'

All repeat: A Scout is friendly and considerate.

Listen to this old proverb, 'A man that hath friends must show himself friendly. There is a friend that is closer than a brother'.

And Jesus said, 'Always treat others as you would like them to treat you: that is the law and the prophets.'

All repeat: A Scout is a brother to all Scouts.

John said about Brotherhood; 'The man who loves his brother dwells in the light, there is nothing to make him stumble. But one who hates his brother, walks in the dark and has no idea where he is going.'

All repeat: A Scout has courage in all difficulties.

David wrote in the Psalms, 'Serve the Lord, be of good courage, and he will strengthen your heart'.

All repeat: A Scout makes good use of his time and is careful of possessions and property.

Paul wrote to Ephesus: 'Be most careful how you conduct yourselves, like sensible men. Make good use of present opportunity and try to understand the Will of the Lord'.

All repeat: A Scout has respect for himself and for others.

Paul, in writing to the Romans said, 'I implore you by God's mercy to offer your very selves to him, dedicated and fit for His acceptance. Don't be conceited or think too highly of yourselves but have equal regard for one another. Discharge your obligations to all men'.
And Jesus said, 'How blest are those whose hearts are pure for they shall see God.'

Hymn
Lord From Whose Hand we Take our Charge (from *Enlarged Songs of Praise* by permission of Oxford University Press).
Tune: *Melita (Eternal Father Strong to Save)*

1. Lord from whose hand we take our charge,
   The care of childhood and of youth,
   To set their feet upon life's road
   In loyalty to right and truth:
   O hear us as of thee we ask
   The strength and wisdom of our task.

2. That we may open doors on life,
   And share the visions that we see
   Of the deep wonder of the world
   And man's heroic history,
   And wake in them the answering chord:
   Give us the skill and patience, Lord.

3. That we may use all law and rule,
   Not rudely to oppress and bind,
   But as the needed discipline
   For freedom of the soul and mind:
   Equipped to face, with fearless eyes
   And steady faith, life's enterprise.

4. That we may understand their need,
    When comes their hour of strain and stress,
    With sympathy to help and save
    From sordid thoughts and bitterness:
    Lord, use our struggles, conflicts, fears,
    To light for them the troubled years.

5. 'Tis ours to give and spend ourselves,
    Nor grudge the labour and the pain,
    To sow the seed of noble worth
    Yet without Thee our toil is vain:
    Great Lord of Life, 'Tis thine to give,
    The quickening breath by which they live.
(lights dimmed)

The Address (spotlight on minister)

Hymn (all lights on)
Sing Hosanna.

Give me joy in my heart, keep me praising,
Give me joy in my heart, I pray;
Give me joy in my heart, keep me praising,
Keep me praising 'til the break of day:

Chorus

Sing Hosanna! Sing Hosanna! Sing Hosanna to the King of
     Kings!
Sing Hosanna! Sing Hosanna! Sing Hosanna to the King.

Give me peace in my heart, keep me resting, etc. . . . . .
Keep me resting 'til the break of day:

Chorus

Give me love in my heart, keep me serving, etc. . . . . .
Keep me serving 'til the break of day:

Chorus

Repeat first verse and chorus

The Scout Promise (all will remain standing and reaffirm the
Promise)

On my honour I promise that I will do my best —
To do my duty to God and to the Queen,
To help other people and to keep the Scout Law.

(all remain standing and say together)

Lord God our Father
We pledge ourselves to serve you, the young and all mankind,
In the cause of justice and peace,

For the relief of want and suffering,
And for the praise of your Name.
Guide us by your spirit; give us wisdom;
Give us courage; give us hope;
And keep us faithful now and always, Amen.
Minister: The Lord be with you.
Answer: And with you also.
Minister: May the peace of God, which is beyond our utmost under-
standing, keep guard over your hearts and thoughts, in
Christ our Lord. Amen.
Minister: Go forth in peace.
Answer: Thanks be to God.

(please sit)

Epilogue (lights dimmed — spotlight on Scout)

I am just a boy
with a lot of dreams
but what's the point
I won't get nowhere
I'm just ordinary
nothing special just
.... ordinary
got no chance in this
world unless you're
.... clever
which I'm not.

Allegri Miserere played once again (spotlight concentrated on cross).

Themes

One of the most common forms of worship we encounter is what
is sometimes referred to as the 'hymn sandwich'. A helpful form of
service when properly used it does, however, require a considerable
amount of thought in construction if it is not to degenerate into a
selection of well-known but unrelated hymns interspersed with over-
used readings, some favourite, but not particularly relevant, prayers,
and a talk which has only a slight connection with one or other of the
elements in the service. A service which does not have a continuous theme running through it will tend to confuse rather than help
the participants. On the other hand, a unified service which seeks
to make one main point or express one set of feelings can be
immensely helpful. Consider, for instance, the way in which people
can be helped and moved by such occasions as Harvest, Christmas,
Lent and Easter services.

There are several ways of applying themes in the construction of acts of worship. One is to maintain a traditional structure and taking a theme like 'children', use hymns, prayers and readings all of which refer to children at some point. The first hymn could be a children's hymn, followed by prayers which express sorrow that so many children in the world are allowed to be victims of the cruelty and selfishness of adults. This could be followed by a hymn of thankfulness for children and prayers of intercession on their behalf. There are many children referred to in the Bible and a reading about one of them could lead into a talk, followed by a hymn expressing a child's sense of joy and wonder at God's creation.

Another alternative is to gather material from varying sources and put it into the most meaningful form for a service irrespective of whether this conforms with conventional patterns.

A traditional structure using traditional material

Here is a possible act of worship based on the theme of 'Gratitude'.

Opening prayer: Open our eyes, Lord, to your glory that we may worship you with glad and thankful hearts.
Hymn: *For the beauty of the earth*
Prayers: Confession: *Scout Prayers* 159. Thanksgiving: *Scout Prayers* 103. Intercession (Prayers for others): *Scout Prayers* 47. Joy: *Scout Prayers* 191. The Lord's Prayer.
Hymn: *When all Thy mercies, oh my God, my rising soul surveys.*
Bible readings: Part of Psalm 107 eg verses 23 to 32. Luke 17:11-19 (the healing of the ten lepers).
Hymn: *We thank Thee, Lord, for this fair earth.*
A talk on the theme of 'Gratitude'
Hymn: *Now thank we all our God.*
Benediction: *Scout Prayers* 57.

This basic structure can be used as a pattern to construct a number of acts of worship on a variety of themes. Material relevant to the chosen theme can be inserted into the appropriate place in the pattern. Some of the more obvious subjects which come to mind are those expressed in the Scout Promise and Law. A person putting together an act of worship according to this pattern will need a reasonable knowledge of the Bible, a hymn book and a copy of *Scout Prayers*. It should be remembered that most biblical passages, most hymns and many prayers can be used to provide material relevant to more than one theme.

One technical point to bear in mind when selecting hymns: avoid choosing those having the same meter and length of verse in the same service, otherwise the worship can appear very monotonous.

A traditional structure using contemporary material

The pattern already described can also be used as a structure for contemporary material. It is possible to use songs chosen by the boys instead of the hymns, secular readings to replace those from the Bible and prayers written by the boys themselves. These prayers will often appear to be very much like poetry; this is not something about which to become alarmed as they are expressions of deep concern for which words are an inadequate medium at the best of times.

Here is an act of worship based on the structures shown above, but using entirely contemporary material.

The theme is 'An aim in life'.

Opening sentence: *Scout Prayers* 3 (v).
Song: *Kum bah yah my Lord.* (Which can be interpreted as meaning 'Come by here, Lord'.)
Prayers: Confession: *Scout Prayers* 157. Thanksgiving: *Scout Prayers* 190. Intercession: *Scout Prayers* 161. Joy: *Scout Prayers* 24. Lord's Prayer.
Song: *When I needed a neighbour, were you there?*
Two Secular Readings: 'Stand outside any factory in Britain on a Friday evening and watch the workers hurrying home as the welcome siren sounds. Men and women run for buses, collect bicycles and cars from the parking areas or trudge home at the end of a long week. But they have the weekend to look forward to, they have been paid, they can relax from the pressures and boredom of shop floor and office, and enjoy themselves for forty eight hours — before it all begins again on Monday morning.' (From *Focus on Christianity: Four Working for Humanity* by Horst Symanowski published by Edward Arnold (Publishers) Ltd.)

'Group Captain Leonard Cheshire was awarded the Victoria Cross not for some single act of bravery, but for a continued succession of them when he led his squadron into action dropping flares to mark targets. Then he flew with the force which dropped the atomic bomb on Nagasaki. This marked the end of the war, but was a turning point for Cheshire, who now set out to work to rebuild lives.

After being involved in a number of projects he tried to found a community living a communal life. One of their houses was called Le Court and was near Liss in Hampshire. The community scheme failed, leaving Cheshire alone with this rambling building. Then came Arthur . . . . Cheshire went to see him in hospital, where the matron explained sympathetically that the man was incurable and that there was no more they could do for him. She hinted, too, that his bed was needed for another case to whom medicine could hold out some hope.

Since the hospital wanted his bed, Cheshire tried desperately to find somewhere congenial for the old man to go instead. He had a horror of a dying man ending his life among people who had no particular or personal feeling for him. Then he saw Arthur and spoke frankly to him.

"I'll take you home with me to Le Court" he offered. "It's up to you, if you'd like to risk it." Arthur said he would like to risk it. Cheshire collected him in his own car, drove him to Le Court, put him into a bed made up with borrowed blankets, having himself carried the man into the house and up the stairs, distempered the walls of the room, rigged up a makeshift bell from the patient's bed to his own room, and then settled down to a new life.' (From *Christian*

Focus: *Twentieth Century People* published by the British Broadcasting Corporation and *Cheshire V.C.* by Russell Braddon published by Evans Brothers (Books) Ltd.)

Song: *There but for fortune.*
Talk: This should demonstrate the contrast between the two passages. The monotonous and apparently meaningless nature of the factory workers' life is contrasted with the sense of fulfilment derived by Leonard Cheshire in devoting himself completely to the care of his fellow human beings. The speaker might then refer to the New Testament evidence that it is often in giving ourselves in service to others that we find meaning and significance in life.
Song: *If I had a Hammer* or *Down by the Riverside.*
Blessing: Scout Prayers 54.

Services without traditional structures

It is possible to construct acts of worship which do not conform to traditional patterns. Those compiling the service should select material which is most appropriate to the theme, and put it together in the most relevant way.

A group of people assembling an act of worship should first of all agree on the purpose of the exercise. Is it the intention that the participants should leave with an overwhelming sense of the goodness and love of God or that they should be feeling sad or chastened at the end of the service? Should they feel happy or should they go away considering how they might usefully help other people? There are a variety of questions which need to be asked before the work of putting together the act of worship can begin.

It should be remembered that drama, music and mime have a place in this kind of worship and while these are discussed in other chapters remember that music is a particularly important aid which can go a long way towards creating the right atmosphere. A service which is intended to be quiet and thoughtful could well begin with a period of silence broken only by the quiet strumming of a guitar, while one ending on a note of joy could effectively end with a group playing *Down by the Riverside.*

If the service is to be held indoors, a record or tape-recording might be more effective than a hymn, a prayer or a reading; Martin Luther-King's *I have a dream* speech for instance, some of the songs sung by Joan Baez or Nana Mouskouri or short extracts from radio and television programmes like *The World at One.* It might even be possible for the boys to record a suitable extract themselves.

If the service is to take place in the evening a few colour slides, perhaps with a tape-recorded commentary backed by appropriate music, can be immensely effective. If the theme of the service is 'happiness', what could be more appropriate than showing a series of slides from the previous year's summer camp, providing that was a happy occasion of course!

Illustration of a service on the theme of 'Friendship'

Poem: *Use and Misuse* by a 14 year old boy.

Why do we bother to go to the Moon?
Why do we bother to spend money on weapons?
God made us to love each other,

Not to destroy each other.
God made us able to swim, run and be active,
To make and paint things;
Not to make weapons to destroy each other.
God made us able to go to school and clubs,
But we have misused these assets.
O God why do we have to hate our fellowman?
Because of his creed and colour?
O God make this a better world
Where everybody loves each other.

Prologue: 'A Scout is friendly and considerate.' The Promise lays down that a Scout should help other people, and this law amplifies what such helpfulness entails. A Scout is friendly in that he accepts a person as he finds him, and accepts him cheerfully, so that the person can *see* that he is accepted. He is considerate in that he takes account of people's feelings, he is polite in his everyday meetings with people. *(Scout Leader's Handbook).*

Reading: Mark 3: 13-19. Jesus calls his friends to be with him.
James 2: 21-25. Deeds and theories.

Song: *A Most Peculiar Man*

Reading: 1 Samuel 19: 1-7 (Jonathan and David are friends, to such an extent that when Saul sought David to kill him, Jonathan intervened for his friend).

Readings: from *Peanuts* — Charlie Brown is depressed because he has no friends. Others come to cheer him up and define friendship for him.

Voice A: A friend is someone who accepts you for what you are.
Voice B: A friend is someone you have things in common with.
Voice C: A friend is someone who likes you even when the other boys are around.
Voice D: A friend is someone who sticks up for you when you're not there.
Voice E: A friend is someone who is not jealous if you have other friends.

Prayer: *Scout Prayers* 99.

Song: *The Family of Man*

Readings: 1. The Face of Loneliness

I've been alone in the world since my dear husband died six months ago. You can't expect people to come and see you very often but it would be nice if they did. There are times I feel sad and unwanted. I feel useless because no one needs me. If I could put my hat on and go out it wouldn't be so bad — but I'm too sick and tired to walk alone. I wish I had someone to talk to and be with all the time. It's no use being old these days, you're just a burden.'

2. The Face of Homelessness

A family with four children paid £5 a week for two rooms in Birmingham. One room was so damp it was totally unusable in the winter and so they lived in the kitchen. The mother slept most nights sitting upright in an armchair with a child in each arm. She said that when they did sleep in the larger room she often found their baby like a drowned rat in the mornings. Twenty-seven people shared the one toilet and one cold water tap. The house was in an appalling condition and there was one family in almost every room.

3. The Face of Prejudice

Everyone is aware that there are a large number of foreigners living in Britain today and that many of them are coloured. Often they come from poor, underdeveloped countries in search of better living conditions, education, and greater opportunities in work, but are they able to find them? Furthermore, many young coloured people were born in the United Kingdom and have as much right to the opportunities in life here as any one of us.

Reading: Ephesians 3: 14-19

Reading: Elizabeth Pilenko was a Polish nun interned at Ravensbrück concentration camp and punished for concealing Jewish fugitives from the hatred of the Gestapo. On Good Friday 1945, just before war ended, Elizabeth was watching the pathetic line of women being led to the gas chambers by the brutal guards. One young woman became hysterical, and Elizabeth succeeded in changing places with her when the guards were not watching.

Reading: John 15: 7-17

Prayer: *Scout Prayers* 75 and 76 and some act of dedication which could be a repeat of the Promise.

Dismissal and Benediction

Whether you decide to use a traditional structure or not, always ensure that your material is in keeping with the overall theme of the service. Keep readings short and to the point. Sometimes short pieces of drama can be more effective than readings; this is particularly true for a generation of young people who have been trained by their culture to respond more quickly to visual imagery than to what they hear. Information on this subject can be found on page 59.

Use of the Scout Promise and Law

Before giving practical hints and suggestions as to the use of the Promise and Law in worship, it is important first to appreciate who they should be included. An opportunity could be taken before an act of worship to explain that the Promise and Law are, in the first instance, a link with God's Law. In the Old Testament we read that God gave the law through Moses (Exodus 19: 10 to 20: 17); this passage contains the Ten Commandments. In the New Testament Jesus expressed that Law in the two great commandments.

"Hear, O Israel, The Lord Our God is the only Lord; 'Love the Lord your God with all your heart, with all your soul, with all your mind, and with all your strength.' That is the greatest commandment. It comes first. The second is like it: 'Love your neighbour as yourself.' There is no commandment greater than these. Everything in the Law and the Prophets hangs on these two commandments."

(St. Matthew 22: 34-40; St. Mark 12: 28-32; St. Luke 10: 25-28).

The Promise and the Law are expressions of the two great commandments in a way that we can all readily understand. That is to say, we do our best to love and serve God (Duty to God); we do our best to be loyal to the Queen and those she represents (Civil Law and authority); we do our best to help others and to keep the Scout Law (Love your neighbour as yourself).

However obvious it may be to some, this understanding is vital before the Promise and Law can be related to the religious found-

ation on which our Movement rests. This can be done in a most practical way by using the Scout salute. In making the salute, one finger is more prominent than the other two. It should remind us of the prime importance of the first promise 'On my honour I promise that I will do my best — to do my duty to God' which is no less than another version of Our Lord's first Commandment.

The other fingers raised in the salute should remind us of the remaining two parts of the Promise. These are related to each other; we owe a duty to the Queen and to her lawful authority, and we also have an obligation within society to make it a happier place for everybody to live in. We should remember that when Jesus was asked which was the greatest commandment of all he gave the first priority to loving God, then went on immediately to say 'love your neighbour as yourself.' In Scouting the second part of the Promise says that we will do our best to 'help other people' and this is the finest contribution Scouts can make to the world in which they live.

The third finger in the Scout salute should remind us of the final part of the Promise 'to keep the Scout Law'. The Scout Laws are simply ways of expressing the behaviour laid down by Jesus. Loyalty to our Laws each day helps us to be conscious of our duty to God and to others.

The Promise and Law are not, then, a vague, meaningless repitition of an out-dated irrelevance, but something concrete and challenging and, in their outworking, a practical guide to daily living. Every morning should begin with this determination to offer our hearts, our souls, our minds and our strength to God in everything we do.

The Promise

The Promise should not be renewed regularly in worship but saved for special occasions. When it is used, as for example at a St. George's Day Service or on some other special occasion, one of the following forms might be appropriate.

1. *The Commissioner says:* (a) The Scout Promise is based upon the great commandments of Jesus. 'Love the Lord your God with all your heart, with all your soul, with all your mind, and with all your strength and love your neighbour as yourself.' Let us then with pride and purpose renew our Scout Promise.

(b) The Cub Scout Promise is based upon the words of Jesus. Let us then renew our Cub Scout Promise.

Scouts

On my honour I promise that I will do my best —
To do my duty to God and to the Queen,
To help other people
and to keep the Scout Law.

Cub Scouts

I Promise that I will do my best —
To do my duty to God and to the Queen,
To help other people
and to keep the Cub Scout Law.

2. The Promise can be led by a suitable person, phrase by phrase, the congregation repeating.

3. After the recital of the Promise,

V. That we will do our best to seek to do our duty to our God with all sincerity and truth.
R. With your help, Lord, we will keep our Promise. Lord make your way plain before me, let your glory be my end, your word my rule, and then, your will be done.
V. That we will do our best to serve our country and our Queen willingly with devotion and love.
R. In your strength Lord, we affirm our Promise. Lord, guide the destiny of our nation, direct those who advise the Queen, and help us all to strive for justice and peace.
V. That we will do our best to help all others, to support the weak, to strengthen the needy, and to learn to love our neighbours as ourselves.
R. In your strength, Lord, we affirm our Promise. Lord, teach us to care.
V. That we will do our best to keep the Law of this Movement that unites us all.
R. In your strength, Lord, we affirm our Promise. Almighty Father, Saviour of us all, give us strength and the will to keep the Promise we have made. Forgive our weakness and uphold us in your power. Amen.

The Law

If it is decided to recite the Law it may be taken at almost any point in an act of worship, but its place should be chosen carefully in relation to the other parts of the service. There are a number of alternatives:
1. At the beginning of the service which would emphasise that Scouts are pledged to a definite code of living and that those present have come together to worship God.
2. In conjunction with a reading from the Bible, especially if the reading has been chosen to illustrate one of the Laws, or if the object is to show how the Scout Law and the Christian life blend into each other.

Suggested Bible passages which illustrate the Laws.

Trust: Matthew 25: 14-23.
Loyalty: Matthew 26: 75.
Friendship: John 15: 12-14.
Brotherhood: John 1: 11-12.
Courage: All accounts of the Passion of Our Lord.
Care: John 10: 12.
Respect: 1 Thess. 4: 1-8.
(Other suitable passages will be found on pages 46 & 48).

3. Following an address or talk. This would be natural if the address is intended to stress one or more of the Laws. In this case, the recital of the Law could be followed by a suitable prayer for

strength to keep the Law as shown below.

The Commissioner or minister: The keeping of our Promise and Law is no easy task. It calls for all that is best in us; our courage, our loyalty, our energy and our power to persevere. But even the best we can do is not enough without God's help. (Here may follow a suitable prayer such as —)
(a)   Lord, help us to be true men and serve you better as the days go by, through Jesus Christ our Lord. Amen.
(b)   (To be said by all)
Lord Jesus I give you my hands to do your work;
I give you my feet to go your way;
I give you my tongue to speak your truth;
You 'grew in wisdom and stature';
Help me to make progress in my understanding of the Promise and Law,
So that I may find favour with God and grow in love for my fellow men. Amen.
(c)   (Using boy participation) *Scout Prayers* 96-100 and 59-61 for Cub Scouts.

4.   At the end of the service. In this case, all that has gone before would lead up to the actual recital of the Law as pointing to the high standard of daily living that Scouting requires and which can be attained only in the strength and grace of God.

Note: The Law need not be recited by one person alone, but proficiency should never be sacrificed for numbers. To recite the Law by heart is usually better in this situation than to read it, but boys who may well be nervous could be given confidence by having a copy in their hand.

The Cub Scout Law
A Cub Scout always does his best,
thinks of others before himself
and does a good turn every day.

The Scout Law
A Scout is to be trusted.
A Scout is loyal.
A Scout is friendly and considerate.
A Scout is a brother to all Scouts.
A Scout has courage in all difficulties.
A Scout makes good use of his time and is careful of possessions and property.
A Scout has respect for himself and for others.

Prayer

Anyone who is called upon to lead prayer, whether in a formal act of worship in church or in an informal setting following a meeting or a camp fire, needs practical help. The disciples' request to Jesus was, 'Lord teach us to pray', and that need is ours also; whether praying alone or leading others, we are always learners.

But what is prayer? Before we can deal with the practical aspects we must say something about prayer itself. It is the name given to the communication between a human being and his god; a two-way process of speaking and listening although, of course, you don't have to make an audible sound in order to 'speak', any more than you have to have ears in order to 'listen'.

There is also an important preparation to prayer that is necessary and which involves a willing offering of oneself to God for his purpose. You are going to be with Him in a special sense and a period of silence is therefore a most important pre-requisite.

A further point needs to be mentioned; there are many folk who never get beyond praying to God in times of emergency or trouble. They think of Him only when they want something for themselves or when no other course is open to them. This is a failure to understand that sincere prayer depends upon a relationship that must be cultivated like an intimate friendship. That is why our first duty is to praise God — unreserved praise is one of the most unselfish acts that we can perform. This should be followed by thanks; for life and its opportunities; for health and strength; thanks, in fact, for everything.

There is room in every prayer for confession, for we are all unworthy and fail even to attain our own highest aspirations, let alone God's Will. To ask for His forgiveness and blessing is a vital element in any prayer. From there we offer ourselves to God asking for the help, strength, courage and faith to live our lives according to His Will. Finally we pray for others and their needs.

Common Problems

No-one will pretend that prayer is easy and whereas the problems of prayer do not come within the scope of this book, it may be helpful to call attention to a few of the common difficulties that people experience.

For some the problem is simply that they don't believe in it. This is because they have no living faith in God, but while this may seem an unsurmountable difficulty, God always listens to those who speak simply and sincerely whatever their beliefs or doubts or fears. Many an unbeliever has found strength in prayer. Our job in all this is to help boys to understand that God is available and approachable at all times and is concerned with even the smallest and simplest of things. God is a personal God and is prepared to listen to everyone.

Others, while having some belief in God, will say that they have never been 'trained' to pray and so it has never been a part of their lives. In this sense God has never been a trusted friend and father, merely a remote and unknown 'being'. This only serves to illustrate the totally inadequate idea of God and of the function and purpose of prayer that many of us have. It may not be our fault, but it is something we can put right. Luther once said that 'Prayer is faith going into action' and that is a very good definition, for to believe in God is not merely to believe that there must be a God of some sort, but to believe that you can enjoy a living and vital relationship with him.

The importance of prayer

Prayer is, in a sense, a mystery we shall never explain. Men have prayed from the earliest of times and no doubt all men pray for one reason or another at some point in their lives. But whatever our personal views, it is an established fact of religious experience that prayer is the highest aspiration of the human personality. No act of worship, be it formal or informal, is complete without it and no religion can properly exist without it. The vital thing to grasp about prayer is that through it, perhaps more than in any other way, we can listen to what God is saying to us.

There are several special occasions such as Investitures, when parents are present at an open evening, at District and Local Association functions, when prayers are usually held at the end and therefore serve as an invaluable reminder that religion is involved with the whole of Scouting. The time spent in camp provides some of the most memorable moments in a Scout's career and as such offers many wonderful opportunities for meaningful worship.

The creation of the right atmosphere is very important. A simple example is that of the camp fire. It is rarely effective to end with an extremely noisy song or yell and then expect everyone to enter into a time of prayer. A camp fire programme should be thought out well beforehand with the more lively and noisy items coming at the beginning and leading to quieter and more thoughtful ones as the fire burns lower, providing a suitable introduction to an evening act of worship which will make a genuine and lasting impression on those present. The same applies to prayers at the end of a Troop meeting. Thought and preparation beforehand are vital.

Preparation

All that has been said above requires that we give as much time and thought to prayers as we give to any other part of our activity. A leader would not go down to a Troop meeting or set out for camp or a hike without having a carefully prepared programme. Training and programme planning are integral to good Scouting. In fact, if you are a good leader you will have in your mind every detail of the evening, of the day or week in question. The matter of Troop prayers must be included with this planning. It is quite wrong to think that by opening a book of prayers at random at the very last moment you will be fulfilling your responsibility. Almost certainly, unless you are a genius, you will fail.

It is important to give the boys an active part in the preparation as well as the service itself, for by sharing this experience they will almost certainly learn something more about the real meaning of worship. Do not forget that a good story is always an excellent way of introducing a time of prayer; so is an acted sequence portraying a Biblical story or a role play. All sorts of resource material can be used to spark off new ideas — ideas from books, recent events, newspapers — even pop songs. One way of making worship more relevant is to take some subject like 'Honesty' or 'Unselfishness', 'Race Relationships' or 'Injustice' and get the boys to work out their own ideas and form them into a theme. This would need guidance and true leadership but is very worth while and would encourage the boys to formulate their own prayers in their own words.

Suitability

It should be obvious, but needs emphasising, that in choosing prayers or making them up, they should be suitable and relevant. This should take into account the ages of those present; you would not use the same prayers for Cub Scouts as you would for a Commissioner's meeting! With Cub Scouts, for example, the subject matter will be varied and very simple. The ideas should come from the boys' experience and this will express itself in personal details. If you understand your boys, you will know what they want to pray about. Don't forget that you are a leader and in many respects a teacher too and you must be prepared to guide them. Remember that what is true of Cub Scouts is also true of all others; prayers must be suitable, simple, relevant and natural.

As Scouts we are part of the world in which we live and we cannot and should not ignore this. We must never seek to build a wall around ourselves and attempt to create something artificial, and therefore our prayers should include our neighbourhood, our town and our country and indeed the whole world as well as the activities of the Group. We must make it plain to our boys that God is concerned with the whole of life and this must be reflected in our prayers.

The very word 'prayers' suggests to some that the meeting must be led by one person or that they must use special words and phrases or speak with a special voice. None of these things is true and the Scout Leader has a wonderful opportunity to break down the formality and artificiality that is often associated with an act of worship. The use of words is important: for most boys the 'Thees' and 'Thous' are 'out'. There is no reason why prayers should not be written in simple and modern English and often those personal feelings which come straight from the heart and from a particular situation are more sincere than those taken from printed sources. All the same, many 'classic' prayers are as suitable and as relevant as the day they were written.

Readings

From early times acts of worship have included extracts from revered writings. History indicates the use of books, letters and sayings of holy men as a means of instruction in doctrine and moral behaviour and to ensure continuity of tradition. For example, we read that the Child Jesus expounded the Scriptures to the elders in the temple at Jerusalem. The Christian religion has always drawn heavily from the books of the Old and New Testament in its worship just as the Koran, the scriptures of Islam, has a special place for the followers of the prophet Mohammed.

The main source of readings in worship for Christians is the Bible. This is really the recording of God's dealings with man; every human situation is there, as relevant to our own times as in the past. The choice of passage will depend much on the individual's knowledge and familiarity with its contents. There are many translations nowadays which use contemporary language.

But bear in mind that the Bible should not be the sole source of readings for worship. Any passage from literature or other secular source which seems to fit into the general context or theme of the service may be used to give added freshness, topicality and relevance. Many suitable extracts can be found in the pages of local and national newspapers. Specific anthologies of readings do exist, eg. *Leadership: selected readings* (C. A. Gibb); *Gathered Together:* readings on religious themes (Oxford University Press); *The Devil with James Bond* (Ann S. Boyd): using themes and situations from the Bond books in association with the gospels. In addition, you may come across in your private reading passages which are suitable for future use. Poetry, particularly 'social' poetry, may strike you as very apt, eg. *People* by Yevtushenko; *Stepney Words* compiled by C. Searle. Publications dealing with school worship or religious education can also be a rich source, eg. *Alive in God's World series; Education through Worship.*

The presentation of the reading can make or mar a service. The choice of reader is important; adequate time must be given for him to become familiar with his text and, if possible, with the actual place from which he will read. Very often familiarity with the microphone and hearing his own voice beforehand in the church or hall will give confidence. It helps to give a brief preamble to the reading, putting it in context or pointing out its relevance; this should be prepared by some competent person. It may be more striking to use two or more readers for a single text, especially where there is narrative and dialogue. A recording, too, of some special address or passage may be more arresting than a 'live' reader.

Short lessons, suitable for Camp Prayers
General
Luke 10: 25-28; The two great commandments.
Phil. 2: 5-8; Christ's humility.
Matt. 5: 13-16; You are the salt of the earth.
Phil. 4: 8-9; Whatsoever things are true, honest, pure.
1 Peter 3: 8-11; Summary of the Scout Law.
1 Samuel 18: 1-5; Jonathan and David. Brotherhood.
John 15: 12-15; No greater love than this.
1 John 4: 7-8, 20-21; Let us love one another.

Lessons appropriate to the Scout Law
1. Trust
Joshua 2: 1-14; Rahab and the scouts.
2. Loyalty
Luke 19: 41-44; Christ's lament over Jerusalem: patriotism.
1 Peter 2: 13-17; Loyalty to the constitution.

3. Friendship
Exodus 2: 16-19; Moses protects the shepherdesses.
1 Peter 3: 7-12; Relationships.
Ecclesiastes 6: 1-17; On friendship.

4. Brotherhood
1 Samuel 18: 1-5; David and Jonathan.
1 John 4: 7-8, 20-21; Let us love one another.

5. Courage
Acts 16: 19-34; Paul and Silas sing in prison.
Acts 27: 20-26; Paul heartens the shipwrecked crew.

6. Care
Ephes. 5: 15-16; Be most careful.

7. Respect
Ephes. 5: 1-14; Walk as children of light.

Passages from the Old Testament
Genesis 22: 1-12; The testing of Abraham.
1 Chron. 11: 15-19; David's friends risk their lives for him.
Ecclesiastes 3: 1-8; A time for everything.
Ecclesiastes 11: 9 to 12: 2; 13-14; Rejoice, young man, in your youth.
Isaiah 40: 1-11; 'Comfort ye, comfort ye my people'.
Wisdom 3: 1-9; For the dead.
Ecclesiastes 44: 1-15; Let us now praise famous men.

Psalms
1: 1-4; 62.   A man who trusts in God.
23.   The shepherd's psalm.
96; 98; 103;
113; 118; 146;   } Praise and thanksgiving.
148; 150.

Main events in the life of Our Lord
The announcement to Mary; Luke 1: 26-38.
The Nativity; Luke 2: 1-7.
The Presentation in the Temple; Luke 2: 21-38.
Jesus at 12 years goes to Jerusalem; Luke 2: 41-52.
The Sermon on the Mount; Matt. 5: 1-16.
The Transfiguration; Matt. 17: 1-10.
The Lord's Prayer; Matt. 6: 9-13.
Palm Sunday Triumphant Entry; Matt. 21: 1-11.
The Last Supper; Matt. 26: 20-29.
                  Luke 22: 14-23.
                  John 13: 21-38.
The Passion;   Matt. 26.
                  Mark 15.
                  Luke 23.
                  John 18 & 19.
The Resurrection; Matt. 28: 1-10.
                  Mark 16: 1-8.
                  Luke 24: 1-12.
                  John 20: 1-18.
The Ascension;   Luke 24: 44-53.

Some miracles of Our Lord
Water turned into wine at Cana; John 2: 1-11.
Miraculous catch of fish in Galilee; Luke 5: 4-11.
The cure of the Centurion's servant; Luke 7: 1-10.
Widow's son raised to life at Nain; Luke 7: 11-17.
The feeding of the five thousand; Mark 6: 30-44.

Lazarus raised to life; John 11: 1-44.
Ten lepers cured; Luke 17: 12-19.

Some parables of Our Lord
The Sower; Matt. 13: 1-9.
The ten talents; Matt. 25: 14-30.
The two debtors; Luke 7: 36-50.
The candle under a bushel; Mark 4: 12-25.
The Good Samaritan; Luke 10: 25-37.
The importunate friend; Luke 11: 5-13.
The Prodigal Son; Luke 15: 11-32.
The publican and the pharisee; Luke 18: 9-14.

Some disclosures of Our Lord
The Beatitudes; Matt. 5: 1-12.
On overcoming evil with good; Matt. 5: 38-42.
On loving your enemy; Matt. 5: 43-48.
On the Door and the Good Shepherd; John 10: 1-21.
How to pray; Luke 11: 1-13.
On forgiveness; Matt. 18: 21-35.
On faith and duty; Luke 17: 5-10.
On the Last Judgement; Matt. 25: 31-46.

Stories and Talks

It is usual, although not essential, to have a story or talk at some point in an act of worship. When a person is invited to speak it should be made clear exactly what is required; he should be told the age range of those who will be taking part in the service, and if a theme has been chosen, he should be told what it is. If possible he should be consulted regarding the planning of the service. Whatever happens, the speaker should be someone who relates well with young people and who knows how to communicate with them. For this reason, the opinions of the Scouts themselves are particularly important in choosing the right person.

A Scout Leader will often be required to give a talk in a Scout act of worship. Some leaders may be daunted by this prospect, and in order to help them the following simple rules are set down for guidance:
1. Decide upon the main point that you wish to make.
2. Think of a series of stories or incidents from real life which illustrate your point.
3. Practise telling the stories.
4. Write down on a postcard a few key words to help you remember the sequence of your talk.
5. Be absolutely clear in your own mind what it is you wish to say: if you are not clear, you will simply end up confusing the listeners.
6. Restrict yourself to a maximum of ten minutes and remember that when you are talking time passes much more quickly than when you are listening.
7. When speaking, stand still and relaxed without shuffling from one foot to the other.
8. Be natural — avoid putting on a special 'holy' voice for the occasion. Talk to the Scouts as you would normally at a Troop meeting.

Stories

The remainder of this chapter consists of a selection of sample stories which could be used on various occasions. In addition to those outlined the Scout Leader should consider telling the stories of great men and women who have lived recently, or who are still alive. These may include people like Dietrich Bonhoffer, Martin Luther King, Chad Varah, founder of the Samaritans, Tubby Clayton, founder of Toc H, Bishop Trevor Huddleston, Anne Frank and Leonard Cheshire. Two very useful books on this subject are *Christians and Social Work* and *Four Working for Humanity*, both written by Ian H. Birnie and published by Edward Arnold.

David and Jonathan

The story falls into several parts:—

1. David meets Jonathan. David, the shepherd boy, slew Goliath, the Philistine, and reported to Saul, the King of Israel. Jonathan was the eldest son of the king; he was a noble, courageous and loyal prince. (I Samuel 18: 1-7). David's successes on the battlefield against the Philistines made Saul jealous.
2. Saul's changeable temper (I Samuel 19: 1-18). David stayed for some time with Samuel, the prophet who had secretly annointed him the future king of Israel when he was a boy.
3. Jonathan helps David (I Samuel 20: 1-43).
4. Jonathan's solemn promise. David lived in hiding for some time (I Samuel 23: 14-18). For several years David fought against the Philistines on behalf of the Israelites and Saul. But he was never certain of Saul and his jealousy. He was forced to live the life of an outlaw and appeared to change sides, although he spent his time organising guerilla warfare against the Amalekites and staving off attacks from Saul. One day the Philistines killed Saul and Jonathan in a battle at Gilboa.
5. David's lament for Saul and Jonathan (II Samuel 1: 1-13, 17-27).

The story of David and Jonathan is the classic biblical one about friendship. It is the story of a friendship which stood the test of many strains and stresses. There was the fact that the boys came from different backgrounds; it was a friendship which met with parental disapproval; the boys were on opposing sides in a feud that nobody wanted.

But the relationship brought out the best in the two boys, rather than the worst. It led to Jonathan constantly trying to make his increasingly paranoic father act with moderation rather than violence; it led to David refusing to be disloyal, even under intense provocation; it led to David refusing to feel proud and glad at the defeat of someone else. Indeed, it could well be that David's future greatness as a King was based on the strong character that was formed in the turbulent friendship with Jonathan.

This next story can be used in a variety of ways, and should be suitably embroidered in various places. The main point with which it deals is the fact that human beings all too easily take things for granted: the love and the friendship of those people with whom we share our lives; all the modern comforts that most people have in a western society — homes, regular meals, hot water and a bed.

It was the week before summer camp and Brian, the Scout Leader, was visiting the homes of all the boys who were to go with the Troop to the camp. He knocked on the door of the house where Barry lived. The boy opened the door, saw Brian and said, "Be careful, my Mum's in a bad mood."

Barry showed Brian into the sitting room where his parents were, and disappeared upstairs to his room. The parents were friendly enough and they talked about all sorts of things. Eventually the subject of summer camp came up. Barry's mother said: "I'll be glad when that boy goes off to camp and gets out of my way — I've never known him be so much trouble as he is at the moment. He comes in with his dirty shoes and leaves mud all over the carpets; he leaves his clothes all over the place and he never helps around the house."

Ten days later, sitting around the fire in the Panther Patrol kitchen, Brian asked the boys if they were enjoying camp; they all said they were. He asked them what they enjoyed most about Scout camps in general. Barry spoke up and said: "Going back home." When asked to explain further, he said, "Well camp is always fun, but the best part is when you get back home and your Mum has a dirty great big plate of sausages, beans and chips for you, and then you can lie and soak in a hot bath and get into bed in between clean sheets in your own room."

Later still, after they'd all returned from camp, Brian was visiting the parents again to see if the boys were all right. When he reached Barry's home the atmosphere in the house was totally different from his previous visit. Barry didn't rush off upstairs out of the way — instead he went into the kitchen to make a cup of tea. His mother couldn't say enough good things about him: "I don't know what you did to him at camp, but he's a changed boy — he appreciates the things I do for him, and he has even started helping around the house; he even says 'thank you' when I give him his dinner. Mind, I missed him when he was away at camp."

The point could usefully be made that it is good for all human beings to stop from time to time and think of the things for which they ought to be grateful. At all costs, avoid allowing listeners to draw from the story the conclusion that the more we 'rough it' at camp, the more will we appreciate our homes. The scene at camp should be described in such a way as to indicate that it was a good, normal, happy camp, which everyone was enjoying.

An appropriate reading to go with the story might be the New Testament story concerning the healing of the ten lepers, only one of whom returned to say 'thank you'.

As a basic illustration of the nature of prejudice, the following story is most suited for older Scouts. There are two kinds of prejudice involved — that of Ian, who won't believe what he reads because he doesn't want to do so, and that of David, who is inclined to believe the story because it reinforces what he has already been led to believe about South Africa. The speaker should spend a little time applying these two kinds of prejudice to issues in his own society to which people react with less than objectivity — issues concerning trade unionism, politics, religion.

David, a seventeen year old Venture Scout, was reading a piece in the newspaper about an incident in Cape Town the previous day. The paper said that a gang of white hooligans had attacked an African when he was waiting for a bus 'because he was too well dressed'; they had pushed him into the gutter, torn his clothes and left him unconscious.

When David had finished reading this paragraph, Ian came into the room. Ian was sixteen, and had recently returned to England after living most of his life in South Africa. David told Ian what he had just read in the paper.

"Serves the bloke right," said Ian.

"What do you mean, serves him right?"

"He shouldn't have interfered, should he?"

"He didn't interfere," said David, getting angry. "Here, read it for yourself." He passed the paper to Ian.

Ian read it. "This is stupid — how can it say that this fellow was just standing there? And why do they call him an African?"

David replied: "Because that's what happened — you got it wrong when I first told you."

Ian thought for a moment, then he said: "I'll tell you what happened. That native stole some money to get some new clothes, and then he walked up the street to try to tell the white people that he was as good as them. He came up to the white men, and tried to push them off the pavement. So they hit him."

It was obvious to Ian that this was the true version. He also recognised that it was different from the version in the newspaper. Then he said: "It's a shame that people in England are so ill-informed about the real situation in South Africa. If you were living there you'd know that the situation described in the paper is not true."

The point should be made that all human beings are prejudiced and interpret other peoples' actions in a way that supports rather than opposes their basic prejudices. If you pass someone you know in the street and he doesn't acknowledge you, a variety of interpretations can be placed on this: he could have been deliberately rude, or he was waiting for you to speak first to be assured that you wished to be friendly, or his mind could have been so much on other things that he didn't notice anyone. The reason that you give will depend on the basic feelings that you have about him — if you dislike him, it'll be the first reason; if you like him you'll give the third reason.

Ask a Scout what he is doing; his answer may be 'learning to bandage cuts'. But is this all there is to it? Has he stopped to consider why it might be good that he should learn to tie bandages? Has it not got something to do with being equipped to help other people?

Another Scout may answer that he is learning the signs on an Ordnance Survey map. He should be encouraged to consider why he is doing this and what benefit it will be in the end.

An American visitor to Liverpool at the beginning of the century saw the cleared site where now stands a cathedral. Intrigued, he approached one of the workmen and said, "What are you doing here?" The man replied, "Can't you see? I'm chipping this stone". Dissatisfied, the American asked another man the same question and he answered, "Earning ten shillings a day". He asked a third man, "What are you doing?" The man replied, "Building a cathedral." He saw the vision of the finished task; the others only the trivialities of the immediate present.

The whole aim of mankind must be to produce just and equal societies in which human beings help and co-operate with one another, instead of fighting and destroying. The aim of Scouting is to make a contribution to this vision of a better world.

As with all these stories, this next one can be used for a variety of purposes, but the most significant point it makes is that it is usually only when we give ourselves to other people that we find friendship and fulfilment.

Robert was seventeen. Last year he moved into Newtown. He had great difficulty in making friends. Most people of his own age already had their circle of friends, and it was difficult for him to join them.

One evening while walking along the deserted main street feeling fed up and angry he passed a small tobacconist's shop owned by Mr. Johnson. Through the window he noticed that there was a small fire in one corner of the shop, but feeling so angry his immediate instinct was to ignore it and let the shop burn down. However, as he walked away he began to think of Mr. Johnson and his family. He didn't know them very well, but then he thought of what would happen if the shop should burn down. This caused him to have a change of heart, and he ran to a telephone box and called the fire brigade.

The next evening Mr. Johnson called to see Robert in order to thank him for saving his shop. He asked him what he did in the evenings, only to be told that he did nothing, as he had no friends. It transpired that Mr. Johnson was the local Group Scout Leader, and the Cub Scout Pack needed some more helpers. Robert admitted to having been a Scout a few years ago, and agreed to go along and help with the Pack. He became involved in the Group's activities and began to build up a new circle of friends.

Robert was unable to make friends in the first instance because he so desperately wanted them. This probably meant that whenever he met people he would be so concerned to please them and create a good impression that he would fail to be genuine, and so people wouldn't like him. When he saw the fire in the shop he was faced with a choice: he could either assert himself by watching the shop burn or by doing something for other people (by calling the fire brigade). He did the latter because he realised what would happen to the Johnson family if their livelihood was taken away. It was a coincidence that Mr. Johnson happened to be the Group Scout Leader, but life is full of coincidence. Once with the Cub Scout Pack he was able to apply himself to doing something useful and thus inevitably a new series of friendships emerged.

The story could be used to say something about the nature of a Scout community — that it should be able to welcome into its number all Scouts and former Scouts, irrespective of colour, class or creed. Although Robert was not able to find acceptance in the community in general, he was able to find it in Scouting.

Visual Aids

Throughout history man has sought to use visual aids in worship; church buildings themselves have been some of the most effective. Developments in church architecture, the presence of statues and of stained glass windows as well as paintings around church walls, have all sought to help ordinary men and women participate more fully in worship. In some Christian traditions, the custom of having clergymen and choir members dressed in a special way during services has been an added help.

In this chapter we shall suggest some of the ways in which visual aids can be used in order to help Scouts enter into worship more fully.

It should be remembered that visual aids can do two things —
1. They can help create the desired atmosphere. They focus the attention of the feelings. Church buildings try to do this. We can compare the atmospheres created by a Roman Catholic church building and a Baptist church building; they are entirely different and some people may find that they can worship in the one and not in the other. It is important to consider how boys react to the atmosphere around them before deciding whether or not it is conducive to worship. It should be remembered that boys are not necessarily helped by a worshipping environment which adults find helpful.
2. They can focus the attention of the mind. A cross or crucifix on an altar can do this, as can the decoration of the church with harvest produce in September and the building of a crib in the church porch at Christmas. It is not an accident that those services in which people find themselves most fully able to participate are also those which are most visually powerful.

Worship in camp

Boys usually like to set aside part of the camp site as a simple chapel where they make a small wooden cross and place it on a tree or a table made from tree trunks. The cross and the table can help the boys to focus their minds when they are taking part in communal acts of worship.

The evening camp fire within a circle of boys provides a setting which itself is a powerful image evoking a feeling of peace. The sentiments expressed in the prayers should naturally build on this experience as should those said in a tent on a wet and windy night, stimulating our sense of being protected from those violent forces in the world which cause us to be afraid.

Worship in the Troop room

Again, it is often helpful to have something on which to focus the attention of the boys when worship is taking place in the Troop room. A simple wooden cross made at camp and hung on the wall will often be all that is required, but if an act of worship is to have a particular theme it is a help if some further visual aid can be provided. For instance, a carol service could take place around a Christmas tree or a crib which the Cubs or Scouts have made. A harvest service could take place around some produce which the boys had collected for a local group of old peoples' houses. During Christian Aid Week the boys could put up a series of pictures obtained from organisations like Oxfam and Christian Aid.

Whenever possible visual aids should be put together by the boys themselves. They can take the form of photographs from magazines and newspapers stuck onto card and pinned on the walls or pictures drawn by the boys themselves, illustrating the theme (eg. friendship, helping other people) of the service. Indoors, it is always possible to use films and colour slides and many charitable organisations produce films illustrating their work which can form a suitable basis for an act of worship. There are a variety of ways in which colour slides can be used: either simply as a stimulus to thought or with a running commentary thus effectively providing an illustrated talk. It may be possible to record a commentary on tape accompanied by appropriate music.

Visual aids in talks

Talks to boys should consist of a few clear illustrations linked together with as little explanation as possible. The more explanation that is required in a talk, the less effective it becomes. Recall how television advertisements often have little or no explanation, but merely present a picture and associate with it the product they are trying to sell.

In a small group of people it is possible for the speaker to have, say, half a dozen large pictures, each illustrating a different part of his talk. He can hang the appropriate picture on the wall behind him, or hold it in front of him, while he is talking about it. These pictures can be cut out of magazines, or obtained from advertisers. It is preferable that the boys should only be able to see one picture at a time, unless the speaker wishes to end up with a series of pictures in front of his audience. At any rate, the boys ought not to be 'ahead' of the speaker by being able to see pictures that he intends to show later in his talk.

It is also possible to use visual effects as aids in talks. The sense of light coming into a dark world can be communicated to a group of Cubs by asking them all to bring a candle to their meeting. The hall can be in darkness except for one candle at the front of the group. One boy lights his candle from this and the flame is then passed on around the room until all the candles are alight.

Music and Drama

The earliest known forms of drama were those of religious worship. As far back as we may go, perhaps two or three thousand years before Christ, there existed in Egypt an Abydos Passion Play. This play celebrated the death and resurrection of the God Osiris. It may, of course, have been merely an expanded form of ritual, for it was from ritual that drama was born.

An integral part of the drama-ritual was music, popularising the worship to the masses with its rhythmical beat. Today music and drama are being associated with religious worship in a similar fashion to the way in which they were used then. We are coming away from the traditional forms of service and thinking more seriously about the sort of approach that will appeal to today's congregation.

Music

Without doubt music has played an important part in Christian worship over the centuries, leaving us with a wealth of material on which to draw. At the same time, Christians and non-Christians alike have used the media to communicate their most fundamental beliefs; from Beethoven to Lennon, all our composers have expressed themselves through words and music, bringing pleasure to millions throughout the world. How sad it would be if we did not take full advantage of the rich pool of musical variety offered to us. Classical, folk, jazz, blues and pop in all their forms can be used with great effect if carefully chosen and wisely related to the theme of the service.

Unity

Essentially, music in an act of worship should be a unifying factor; something in which the whole congregation can participate, whether listening to a recording of the *Allegri Miserere* to create an atmosphere of peace before the start of the service, or joining in a rousing hymn, *Thine be the Glory, Risen Conquering Son*.

Music is a medium capable of arousing our deepest emotions and is therefore worthy of respect and good use. It should not be used merely to hang the service together, the odd hymn thrown in simply because nothing else can be found that fits.

Which music?

There is no reason why traditional and modern forms should not be used during the same service. For instance, the *Lord's Prayer* could be sung as a solo by a Venture Scout to the well known and now somewhat traditional Caribbean setting, or the choir could sing the *Gloria* to the tune of Beethoven's *Ninth Symphony (Choral)*, fourth movement, *Ode to Joy*. The version shown here was written by the Rev. Paul Jobson and set to music by L. Kercher.

Glory be to God on High
Over all the earth be peace
We praise you and bless you,
Worship you and glorify you
We give thanks to God for your great glory
Lord the true God,
Heavenly King
God the Father Almighty,
Glory be to God on High.

Lord you are the only son
Jesus whom we call the Light
Lord you are the only son
Jesus whom we call the Christ
O Lord God, the Lamb of God,
Son of the world-and-the-Father,
You who free us from all sin,
Show your mercy upon us.

You who free us from all sin
Hear our prayer and give us strength
You have conquered fear and death,
You are high and lifted up —
Raised above all time and space —
Triumphant now and crowned with joy —
You we call our Lord and King,
Glory be to God on High!

In the same service, the congregation could sing *Come and Praise the Lord our King* to the tune of *Michael Row the Boat Ashore*, as the

call to worship. Caribbean, classical and folk music — all used in the context of one act of worship and it has been done!

Which instruments?

There is no reason why a group of young people should not play during a service. Scout acts of worship are basically for young people and so it is better if they can express themselves in their own way. At the same time, the organ is not an instrument to be disregarded simply because it makes rare or fleeting appearances in the pop charts. Indeed, many modern singers and groups are backed by an organ of one kind or another and organ music can be beautifully augmented by other instruments such as the trumpet. How magnificent it would sound if the organ, playing a rousing hymn, could be joined by trumpets from the local band. If well prepared and rehearsed the effect could be breathtaking.

'Praise Him in the sound of the trumpet; praise Him upon the lute
and harp
Praise Him in the cymbals and dances; praise Him upon the strings
and pipe
Praise Him upon the well tuned cymbals; praise Him upon the loud
cymbals.'

Yet somehow, in our worship as Christians, we have forsaken the use of many instruments; perhaps now is the time for their return. A Salvation Army band could make a great contribution to the success of any service — given adequate notice and time for rehearsal. A roll of drums — even the peal of a bell lyre (if these instruments are available), can add tremendously to the overall impact of the act of worship.

All this having been said, it is as well to remember that opinions on new forms of worship — just as with the traditional ones — vary considerably. It is wise, therefore, to ensure that the hymns and music used really reflect the theme of the service, thus whatever the feeling of the congregation, they will see the sincerity of the service in the worship of God.

The Occasion

Occasion is also a guide to the sort of music and hymn to be used. A service in a cathedral will obviously be different in content from that held at a Scout camp, and while the cathedral will perhaps inspire the ceremony and dignity of the organ and the rousing hymn, the countryside will encourage the use of guitars and folk music.

A Choir

A choir is the backbone of the weak voiced congregation and the unknown hymn. Many people maintain that it is best to stick to familiar hymns because this ensures that the congregation will do justice to the words and music. Often the fact that boredom, just as much as ignorance, can kill the effect and joy of a service is ignored. New hymns should certainly be tried and to make sure that the congregation are at least aware of them, hold a short rehearsal just before the start of the service. Once they are known, modern hymns can be just as effective and stirring as old standards.

Recordings

Recorded music can also be used to good effect. Imagine the *Shepherd's Song of Thanksgiving* from Beethoven's *Sixth Symphony* played as an introduction to an annual St. George's Day Service as the flags and colours progress through the church. If the theme is simply 'joy', what more fitting music to start the whole thing off.

Prayer

Meditation or silent prayer during a service can be helped by the playing of a record — Gregorian Chants especially lend the right kind of atmosphere.

Film Music

From time to time film music produces something of interest in this field. Either original compositions or classical music of a special kind are brought to our attention by the popularity of a film. An example of this is the theme music of *2001, A Space Odyssey*, which popularised Richard Strauss' *Thus Spake Zarathustra* — this is an ideal piece for a service based on 'the future'.

Drama

Drama and religion have often been in conflict but today they are drawing close once more. Despite this, many of us think of drama as an embarrassment, and while we can enjoy the theatre, the cinema, the television or the radio, when we are personally required to join in we imagine ourselves as trees hopping around a room or clouds drifting in a sky of self-consciousness. But if we reflect, this is often the way we feel about worship. We are embarrassed about going to church, shy about singing, reserved about praying in front of our friends and neighbours.

Drama in the church

At one time drama was part of the church service; in the Middle Ages something resembling drama was instituted in the church itself. The Holy Communion, which had early developed as a central element in the service of the church, had a certain dramatic feature, particularly on certain days when new elements were added which increased the dramatic significance. Out of this came the presentation by voices chanting in Latin of certain crucial scenes from the Christian story, such as those of the Birth and Resurrection.

A simple play would have gone as follows — the scene would be set from the Bible, in this case the three Marys learn of the Resurrection, and the parts would be acted by priests.

One priest, playing the part of an angel, sits near the altar where a cloth has been laid over the cross representing the sepulchre. The three Marys approach and the angel addresses them:

"Whom do you seek at the sepulchre, Christian women?"

"Jesus of Nazareth who was crucified, O Heavenly One."

Raising the cloth, the angel replies:

"He is not here. He is risen even as He said. Go announce that he has risen from the sepulchre."

This was called liturgical drama, a form of medieval play wherein the dialogue and the movement formed part of the liturgy or service of the day. Today drama has two connections with worship. As a

59

form of ritual it still exists in the Mass, and as an expression of feeling or event it represents an immediate form of worship.

Worship through drama
Undoubtedly the use of drama will not appeal to all leaders, but for those who need convincing as to its purpose and validity, it remains for them to consult those who are, with great success, teaching drama in our schools today. Their feelings and reactions will give the leader something to work on if he is considering drama as an ingredient for his act of worship.

Drama in education is seen as an ideal method of expressing the feelings and concerns of those involved. For example, in the primary school many children have fears of the dark or of thunderstorms. If they are able, with the aid of their teachers, to work up a drama about their fears using both music and movement which they enjoy, then they may come to terms with their fears. This will also apply throughout secondary education, when adolescents are able to act out their fears and aggressions; police drugs raid, a car accident, older youths picking on a younger boy. Participation goes a long way towards understanding.

We can now compare this with worship. Drama helps people to experience situations which they may not otherwise face, or understand. What good is worship of a God who is unknown — belief in God comes through experience of Him. Children who take part in a Nativity Play are in their own way experiencing the birth of Christ. A group of boys acting the betrayal of Jesus are experiencing the feelings of the disciples.

As many people as possible should participate in every act of worship and when we speak of drama in these terms we are not talking about a play on the stage, ceremoniously rehearsed and presented, but a true and immediate expression of the beliefs of those involved.

Dramatic worship in the weekly programme
Cub Scout Pack: The Pack is the ideal place to start using drama since Cub Scouts are usually full of self-confidence and a wish to express themselves. Here is some idea of the kind of format a Christian act of worship could take during an ordinary Pack meeting.

Akela reads to the Pack the story of Jesus' last entrance into Jerusalem and the Last Supper. Then he talks to the Pack about the story and they can ask questions. Finally they discuss how this story could be presented. To do this they must think of what the characters were like, what they felt, what they did and what they wore.

Then Akela plays a record — part of the *Missa Luba* (a Congolese version of the Mass) would be ideal, with plenty of rhythm. The Cubs decide how the story best fits the music and Akela gives each Six part of the story to act. They listen again to the music and then an assistant takes each Six away to rehearse their part. Gradually the drama is pieced together. The words can come spontaneously or the scenes may be mimed.

This sort of drama could easily follow some other story such as David and Goliath, Mohammed and his early followers, or anything else familiar to the Pack, and a series of books by William Martin and Gordon Vallins called *Exploration Drama* will be of particular value in this context.

The Troop: We should turn now to the Troop meeting where a more sophisticated drama emerges. An act of worship begins with some thought provoking readings; perhaps newspaper clippings about the current international or social problems. Each excerpt is read by a different voice. Then there can be a folk song; possibly a protest one allied with the readings.

The Scouts can then decide how they want to put over the message they are trying to convey in some sort of dramatic presentation. Perhaps a scene that they have experienced in ordinary life will illustrate this in the way they want; the important point is that the content should be spontaneous. This can be followed by the Lord's Prayer. A choral presentation of a prayer or reading could be another item. Group verse speaking is a form of drama not often used because it tends to become a chant intoned by a mass of swaying bodies, but any prayer, hymn or dramatic poetry can be brought alive by acting certain scenes.

Always allow the Patrols to plan their own presentation. First of all give the Patrol Leaders an idea or theme, for example 'betrayal', and then allow them to go away and plan their own act of worship with their Patrols.

Theme — Betrayal

If we take this theme we can find plenty of ideas to weave into an act of worship. The Scouts can collect newspaper clippings illustrating an act of betrayal, such as a traitor selling secrets to a foreign power. These can be read out loud, followed by a dramatic presentation of Jesus' betrayal by Judas in the garden of Gethsemane. Then the Scouts could choose their own prayer or perhaps make one up for the occasion.

Introduce plenty of music and singing, both folk and hymns — even a record to listen to, or perhaps the choral presentation of some verse. Many good examples can be found in modern poetry books in your local library; one on the theme 'betrayal' is *Ballad* by W. H. Auden (to be found in the Penguin book *Poetry in the Thirties*). This has a good rhythm to keep the verse going and is a story of a man betrayed to the soldiers by his wife. When the chorus reaches its climax, sound effects could add to the dramatic presentation and you might even find a record which will fit in with the verse.

Here is another example of a possible service.

Theme — Resurrection

A Scout begins by reading the Resurrection story from *The Bible*; the *New English Bible* would probably be the most appropriate version. Then some of the Scouts perform part of the story. This is followed by a dramatic group reading, using three voices, of the Dylan Thomas poem *And Death Shall Have No Dominion*.

The Scouts read prayers and everyone joins in singing Easter Hymns.

These are only rough examples of possible programmes for acts of worship and they are both Christian. You must remember to include all the religions represented in your Troop. If there are any Scouts with religions you do not really know about, then ask them to tell the Troop about their faith and perhaps bring along some of their traditional symbols. They may be able to tell a story of their God which could be turned into a dramatic presentation and featured in an act of worship.

In all worship try to introduce as much music and movement as possible so that the Scouts do not lose interest in what is going on. Use music that the Scouts enjoy and not your own particular favourites. Having once broken the barrier by doing an act of worship like this they will probably have plenty of ideas for next time.

The simplest of everyday occurrences illustrate something of religious or moral significance: discuss this with your Scouts and they will find many instances which can be enacted at the direction of the storyteller, or may be paralleled by events from the Bible. Involve everyone, leave no-one out. Every Scout should have a part, however small, in what is going on. This is a golden rule and there should never be any exceptions.

The Unit: Venture Scouts are more ready to discuss their religious beliefs than the younger age groups in other sections of the Movement, and this should be turned to good advantage. Their act of worship can take as unusual a format as they can decide upon. It may include an excerpt from a modern play — it may involve another *Superstar* or *Godspell* — but it will need more thought and planning than any other act of worship. It will ask more questions and demand more answers. It may not be about any of the current controversial topics — war, pollution, loneliness — but simply be a search for personal belief. *Prayers of Life* by Michel Quoist provides many thought provoking themes. Perhaps some new folk songs will be the hymns. No specimen programme can be given here since this act of worship should be completely new.

Dance

Dance/drama can take many forms, but its principle function in the context of worship is to worship with the body. Dance links the other two forms of worship we have talked about, since it incorporates both music and drama. Many boys find it difficult to communicate their praise of God by singing hymns or saying prayers whereas they can find an expression of their true feelings in the movement of the body. Just as the French are known for the gestures which accompany their speech, so dance is a true expression of feeling or emotion. The show and film *Jesus Christ Superstar* illustrate this very well.

The dance should fit the theme of the service. Supposing this is 'the Resurrection', we can see how this could develop. The ideas, movement and music must be joined together successfully and the dance should be well rehearsed.

1. Ask the boys to tell you the story of the Resurrection and make sure that each point is clear, starting perhaps with the burial of Jesus and moving on to the visit of the women to the tomb and their meeting with the angel; the two on the road to Emmaus; the appearance of Jesus at the disciples' supper.

2. Discuss the sort of emotions and feelings during these events — the grief of the burial; the disbelief and amazement of the women at the tomb; the dawning realisation on the road; the final belief and happiness of the disciples.

Dance should be used wisely; there may be some boys who are afraid to use it to express their feelings and there will be some who see it as an ideal opportunity to play about. If you are not sure how to tackle this ask some suitably competent person such as a movement or drama teacher to help you.

Many of our acts of worship are District functions including all sections of the Movement and in this case something from each should be included. Perhaps the Cubs could say some prayers they have written in their Pack meetings, or perform a short dramatic presentation. The Scouts could read items of news and do some group verse speaking. The Venture Scouts could provide the music and folk songs. The same principle applies here — everyone should join in and there should be a strong theme running throughout which unites the whole.

Flag Procedure

General Considerations

Most, if not all, Scout Troops and Units possess colours. Both the Union Flag and the Troop colour are used frequently at church services, Scouts' Own Services, investitures, parades and in camp. While current practice varies considerably throughout the country, the following points are set out for the guidance of Scout and Cub Scout Leaders.

Flag Procedure

In the Scout Movement, the following procedure should be adopted when the Union Flag is hoisted, broken or lowered:

Hoisting. When the Union Flag is hoisted or broken all present should be brought into the horseshoe or other formation round the flag, except in very large camps. The order should be given, *Troop alert, salute.* On the word *salute*, the Scout carrying out the actual hoisting or breaking proceeds with the matter. The salute ends when the Scout Leader brings his hand down from the salute position, but the Scouts remain at the alert until the Scout who has performed the ceremony has taken two paces back, faced the flag and has saluted, then re-taken his place in the horseshoe. The Scout Leader then gives the order *Scouts, at ease.*

Lowering. When the flag is lowered, the following procedure should be adopted. The attention of all those present in the Troop room or in camp should be called by some suitable sign — in camp the blowing of a horn, the ringing of a bell, or something of that nature. All Scouts, whatever they may be doing, cease operations and come to the 'Alert' facing the flag. The flag is then lowered and when this is done the signal previously given is repeated so that everyone may carry on with their normal duties. It is the custom in the Scout Movement that no-one salutes when the flag is lowered. Those responsible for lowering the flag should take the utmost care to see that no part of it comes into contact with the ground.

In Great Britain the Union Flag takes precedence over all other flags and in camp is flown above all other flags, banners etc. But if British Scouts camping in a foreign country wish to fly that country's flag as a compliment, this should be flown on a separate mast at the same height as the Union Flag.

Flag Carrying — On the March

Slope: Sloped over right shoulder, flag gathered in right hand, left arm swinging free.

Carry — gathered in : Flag gathered in, pole vertical, butt in carrier, held in right hand, back of hand to front level with mouth, elbow square and level with hand, left arm swinging free.

Carry — flying free: Position of hand as in *Carry,* but flag not gathered in.

Use: The *Slope* is the normal method. The *Carry — gathered in* used when marching past or when specially ordered. The *Carry — flying free* is the salute at the actual moment of passing the saluting point. Flags are never lowered on the march.

Note: The attitude of the *Carry* is tiring and should be used sparingly.

At the Halt

Order: Flag held vertically at the right side, butt on ground, gathered in right hand.

Carry — gathered in: As on the march but left arm to side.

Carry — flying free: As on the march but left arm to side.

Lower: Point of pole on ground, pole under right arm and flag free, except when ground is wet or muddy.

Use: The *Order* is the normal position. The *Carry — gathered in* or *Carry — flying free* is used on occasions such as an inspection, when ordered. The flag is lowered as a salute in accordance with *Policy, Organisation and Rules.* When parading with other bodies, common sense should be used in departing from these rules. For example, on Remembrance Day in many places, the British Legion lower flags during the sounding of the Last Post. Scouts should conform. Similarly in International Parades, it is normal custom to follow the practice of the host nation.

Further uses of flags

Seeing that the Union Flag represents the Queen's Colour on parade, it is usual for the Queen's Colour to precede all others. When flags are carried into church, they are usually carried to the minister who receives them from the bearers, either standing or kneeling, according to custom. If handed over kneeling, it is usual to bend the right knee. This allows the 'carrier' or 'bucket' to be in the right position. Each church usually has its own procedures regarding the positioning of the colours after they have been received by the minister. Flags, however, should not be placed on the altar or communion table in normal circumstances. The exception is when a new colour is to be dedicated or blessed.

A general rule underlies all that has been written above, namely that when colours are paraded in the open, in a church, or in a Scout room or hall, all should be done decently and in order so that due respect is given to the symbols of the Movement. For this reason it is normal procedure for Scouts to stand at the Alert as a token of respect when flags are carried in and out of a church, or on and off parade.

Dedication and Blessing of Flags

New flags

The acquisition of a new flag, whether a Troop, Unit or Union Flag, calls for a ceremony of some kind. This may take the form of a simple presentation by the donor, a church service or part of a church service. In consultation with the minister, it might be more appropriate for the act of dedication and blessing to take place during a regular family service of the church. In any case, and particularly where the Group is sponsored by or attached to a local church or religious community, leaders are urged to consult well beforehand with the minister, the County Chaplain or the leader of the religious community concerned. In this way, much confusion can be avoided.

There is no set pattern or ceremony which must be followed. As circumstances vary consultation beforehand is vital so that what is finally agreed is meaningful and clear.

Thought, therefore, should be given to the following points —

1. **Consecration** — Scout and Union Flags should not be 'consecrated' because this means 'making holy'; that is, setting a person or a thing apart for the sole service of God. Hence a church is consecrated because it is to be used solely for the purpose of religion and worship.

2. **Dedication** — this means 'setting apart for a particular purpose', not necessarily religious. An author may dedicate his book to a relative or friend; a church may dedicate a piece of furniture or an organ to God. A gift so dedicated should, therefore, be treated reverently and with respect.

It is, therefore, appropriate in certain circumstances for new colours to be dedicated within the context of a church service, a Scouts' Own Service or in a Scout hall, or for that matter, in camp. It must be remembered, however, that flags so dedicated must be treated thereafter with special care. While all colours should be treated with due respect, opinions differ regarding the exact treatment which should be accorded to dedicated flags and how they should be disposed of when their usefulness is at an end.

Scout Headquarters does not lay down any hard and fast rules, other than — 'If flags are dedicated they must be treated with the greatest reverence at all times; for instance, it would not be correct to fly a dedicated Union Flag on a flagstaff in camp, or to move it uncased without an escort. Groups are advised to consider this carefully before undertaking the charge of dedicated flags.'

3. **Blessing** — a further method is open to Scout Groups depending upon their Sponsoring Authority or their church allegiance. A service of 'blessing of colours' in no way restricts their future use and they may be paraded at the Groups' discretion. The blessing of a colour may become a visible sign of our Duty to God. This is equally true, of course, of a dedicated colour.

There are some who would argue that 'dedicated' is more appropriate in relation to people, and that 'blessing' is better used in relation to things. Both words, in fact, have within them similar or associated implications.

In asking God to bless something we are requesting that it may be put to some good use and that our possession of it may remind us of God. In offering a flag to God, we are making use of symbolism, and its usefulness is to remind us of what it means. The Union Flag is a symbol of our loyalty and service to the Queen, our Country, and our fellow citizens. The Scout Flag is a symbol of our together-ness in Scouting and reminds us of the ideals set out in our Promise and Law. When we bring these symbols to God for his blessing we are asking him to accept this loyalty, service and togetherness and to acknowledge that without his blessing we should not be able to keep our Promise and Law. Bound up with any blessing of flags must go a dedication of ourselves.

4. Planning a ceremony involving the dedication or blessing of flags.

Such planning should be done in consultation with the minister conducting the service. He will be in a position to help in the selection of suitable readings, prayers and hymns. It is strongly recommended that everyday English be used so that all the boys concerned can understand the meaning and purpose behind the service.

The actual ceremony may take place either during the course of an ordinary church service or it may be held separately. Before the service begins, adequate preparation must be made to see that the flag is placed on a stand or table at the chancel steps or some other equivalent position. A colour party consisting of a bearer and two Scouts should be in a convenient position to receive the flag at the appropriate time.

Forms of service

The following are intended as a guide and are not exclusively for the use of Scouts. The wording should be changed according to the occasion. Alternatives are provided for Scout or Union Flags.

(a) **The presentation of flags** — Introduction for a Scout Flag

Minister: (Brother) Scouts, you have come here to receive the flag of your Troop. This flag is a symbol of the unity of the Troop which is part of the world-wide brotherhood of Scouts. As mem-bers of that brotherhood, you are bound together by the Scout Promise which shows that you acknowledge God as the ruler of all men and things; that you pledge your service and loyalty to your Queen and Country; that you are always ready to help your neigh-bours; and that you will strive to keep the Scout Law.

The Scout Flag has a long and honoured tradition and the privi-lege of carrying it is now entrusted to you and to future generations of Scouts in this Troop. It is fitting, therefore, that you should make your Scout Promise again to show your intention of being worthy of of that trust.

Here follows the Scout Promise

Alternative introduction for a Scout Flag

Minister: (Brother) Scouts, we have come together to offer this flag and all that it stands for to God; and to offer ourselves in loyalty

69

and service to Scouting throughout the world. We therefore, dedicate ourselves anew for God's service and purpose for all men, and pray that God will keep us true and loyal to him.

For a Union Flag
Minister: (Brother) Scouts, you have come here today to receive a new Union Flag. This new Queen's Colour is a symbol of our loyalty under God to our Queen and our Country. A great company of men and women have honoured this flag and it is now being handed to you and to future generations of Scouts in the expectation that you will do the same.

(b) Prayers
Suitable prayers could follow, such as:
Minister: God our Father, we ask your blessing upon those who will follow this colour now committed to their charge. Make them worthy to be called your sons and may they always find in you the courage and faith to justify this trust; through Jesus Christ our Lord. (Here may follow the Lord's Prayer).

For a Union Flag
Minister: Lord God, we ask your blessing upon our Country and Commonwealth; upon your servant Elizabeth, our gracious Queen and Ruler; and upon all who are set in authority under her. Grant that we and all who honour this flag may live and work for the good of others in glad obedience to the example and command of your Son, Jesus Christ our Lord, who died in the service of men and who now lives for evermore.

(c) A brief address

(d) The minister will then proceed to the **dedication or blessing of the flag,** using words such as the following:
Minister: According to the faith we hold, we dedicate this flag, that it may be a sign of our duty to God and to our Troop, in the name of the Father, and of the Son, and of the Holy Spirit. Amen. (The final words expressing the name of the Trinity may be excluded where other faiths are concerned.)
or *Minister:* In the faith of the Lord Jesus Christ, we dedicate this flag that it may be a symbol of our duty to God and to our Troop in the name of the Father, and of the Son, and of the Holy Spirit.

For a Union Flag
Minister: In the name of the Father, and of the Son, and of the Holy Spirit, we dedicate and set apart this Union Flag, that it may be a sign of our duty to our Queen and Country in the sight of God.

(e) Further prayers
Further prayers may be added here for our Country, for peace, for Scouting, and any others which may be appropriate.

(f) Presentation of the flag to the Troop
The colour party will advance and receive the flag(s) at the hands of the donor or the minister, the bearer(s) kneeling on the right knee.

Minister: On behalf of your Troop accept this flag which has been dedicated to God, remembering the purpose for which it is dedicated, the cause of which it is the symbol and the honour in which it is to be held.

(g) **The National Anthem** (If desired and particularly where a Union Flag is involved).

(h) **A prayer of dismissal**
This could be a form of the Benediction or Blessing or The Grace.

A simple presentation in a church

The colour is brought to the communion rail, or to a central position in the church, by the bearer.

Minister: This colour is the sign and emblem of our Troop. It represents the honour and code of the Troop, and should always be treated with reverence. We dedicate it to God who is the Lord of our lives and of this Troop.

In the faith of our Lord Jesus Christ, I dedicate this colour that at all times it may be the sign of the .... Troop and an acknowledgement of the allegiance of its members to God; in the name of the Father, and of the Son and of the Holy Spirit. Amen.

Then the company shall say: Almighty God, we pray that this colour may always inspire us to be true to our Promise, loyal to our leaders and obedient to you; through Jesus Christ our Lord. Amen.

The colour is then placed near the communion table.

At the end of the service the bearer kneels to receive the colour, and as it is returned the minister says: Receive this colour on behalf of your Troop. Remember that it has been dedicated to the service of God. Let it be respected by you. Let it be a symbol of loyalty to your Troop and to your Movement the world over.

A simple presentation not in a church

If a church service is felt to be inappropriate (eg, in an Open Group with no specific church allegiance) a simple ceremony may be held in the Group room or in the open air. This does not have to be 'non-religious' because it is not being held in a church building, and any of the forms of words may be used as in the foregoing section. On the other hand, such a ceremony can be more spontaneous and free. Simplicity and sincerity are the key-note.

The following is suggested as being suitable for the presentation of both the Scout Flag and the Union Flag.

The Troop should be drawn up in horse-shoe or open-square formation facing the Scout Leaders and the donor (if present). If the donor is not present, he may be asked to nominate someone to present the flag on his behalf, or the District Commissioner may be invited in his stead.

After a few words of introduction by the Scout Leader, including thanks to the donor, he brings the Troop to the alert. The Scout Leader may lead the Troop in the Scout Promise. The colour party is then called forward and the donor (or his nominee) presents the flag. If the flag being presented is the Union Flag, the National Anthem could be sung.

The Troop stands to the alert as the flag is marched off.

Note: Exact wording has been omitted in order to give the Scout Leader the opportunity of speaking naturally and sincerely in words of his own choosing. The ceremony might well be used at a meeting and the Troop may feel it desirable to invite parents and supporters. If further prayers are needed they may be found in *Scout Prayers*.

Laying up of flags

This is a matter for local initiative and consultation with the minister. Such a service should be short. The ceremony of laying up colours may be preferable during a normal church service. Prayer and the spoken word very much depend upon local conditions.

What has already been said about the dedication or blessing of flags applies also to the laying up of flags. Flags should always be treated with respect because they symbolise important ideals and commitments. That is why we are able to offer them in the first place. It is important that Scouts should understand that this respect derives rather from what they symbolise than for the fact that they are dedicated or blessed.

A final point should be made at the end of this chapter. If any religious service is to be meaningful to the boys attending, it must be well planned and geared to their understanding, regardless of whether it is a Scouts' Own Service, a full ceremonial service in a church, or a simple service of blessing in the open air. Sincerity, simplicity and reality are all keynotes to success.